How to Design a Small House

How to Design a Small House

50 Things to Know
and 4 Examples

David Holowka

The information and advice contained in this book are based on the research and personal and professional experiences of the author. They are not intended as a substitute for consultation with local building officials, or professionals in the fields of architecture, engineering, construction, or finance. The publisher and author are not responsible for any adverse effects or consequences resulting from the use of this book's suggestions, procedures, or examples.

Copyright © 2020 by David Holowka

All rights reserved. No part of this publication may be reproduced, scanned, uploaded, stored in a retrieval system, or transmitted, in any form or by any means, electronic, mechanical, photocopying, recording, or otherwise, without the prior written permission of the publisher.

Published by Small House Lab, New York
www.SmallHouseLab.com

Requests to publish work from this book should be sent to SmallHouseLab@gmail.com.

Photo credits are on page 147.

"Apprehensions" from COLLECTED EARLIER POEMS by Anthony Hecht, copyright © 1990 by Anthony E. Hecht. Used by permission of Alfred A. Knopf, an imprint of the Knopf Doubleday Publishing Group, a division of Penguin Random House LLC. All rights reserved.

Publisher's Cataloging-In-Publication Data
(Prepared by The Donohue Group, Inc.)
Names: Holowka, David, author.
Title: How to design a small house : 50 things to know and 4 examples / David Holowka.
Description: First edition. | New York : Small House Lab, [2020] | Includes bibliographical references.
Identifiers: ISBN 9781734422313
Subjects: LCSH: Small houses—Design and construction. | Small houses—Philosophy.
Classification: LCC NA7533 .H65 2020 | DDC 728/.37—dc23

Library of Congress Control Number: 2019920798

First Edition

Book design by Kevin Woodland

To Mary Ann, Jim, and the memory of our parents

Contents

Introduction 1

1 **Demographics** 12
2 **Architects** 14
3 **Prefabs** 16
4 **Tiny Houses** 18
5 **Money** 20
6 **Site** 22
7 **Footprint** 24
8 **Stories** 26
9 **Accessibility** 28
10 **Basement** 30
11 **Garage** 40
12 **Porch** 42

13 **Trees** 44
14 **Living** 46
15 **Terrace** 48
16 **Entrance** 50
17 **Bedroom** 52
18 **Kitchen** 54
19 **Bathroom** 56
20 **Storage** 58
21 **Door** 68
22 **Window** 70
23 **Window Wall** 72
24 **Space Traps** 74
25 **Alcove** 76
26 **Furniture** 78

Example A
32

Example B
60

27	White 80	41	Served and Servant 124
28	Night 82	42	Thickened Wall 126
29	*Walden* 84	43	Diagram 128
30	Contentment 86	44	Privacy 130
31	Evolution 96	45	Time 132
32	Prospect-Refuge 98	46	Grandeur 134
33	Primitive Hut 100	47	Passion 136
34	Pavilion 102	48	Modernism 138
35	One-Room Appeal 104	49	Timelessness 140
36	Box 106	50	Less Is More 142
37	Box Breaking 108		
38	Endlessness 110		Selected Bibliography 145
39	Boundary 112		Photo Credits 147
40	Clarity 114		

Example C
88

Example D
116

The door of the cavern was big enough to roll a hogshead in, and on one side of the door the floor stuck out a little bit, and was flat and a good place to build a fire on. So we built it there and cooked dinner. We spread the blankets inside for a carpet, and eat our dinner in there. We put all the other things handy at the back of the cavern. Pretty soon it darkened up, and begun to thunder and lighten.... Directly it begun to rain, and it rained like all fury, too, and I never see the wind blow so. It was one of these regular summer storms. It would get so dark that it looked all blue-black outside, and lovely; and the rain would thrash along by so thick that the trees off a little ways looked dim and spider-webby; and here would come a blast of wind that would bend the trees down and turn up the pale underside of the leaves; and then a perfect ripper of a gust would follow along and set the branches to tossing their arms as if they was just wild; and next, when it was just about the bluest and blackest — *fst!* it was as bright as glory, and you'd have a glimpse of treetops a-plunging about away off yonder in the storm, hundreds of yards further than you could see before; dark as sin again in a second, and now you'd hear the thunder let go with an awful crash....

"Jim, this is nice," I says. "I wouldn't want to be nowhere else but here."

Mark Twain, *The Adventures of Huckleberry Finn*

Outside he could hear the tossing noise of the trees, and the teakwood table in the hall — that famous barometer — made a creaking sound. Then, before the rain began, the old place appeared to be, not a lost way of life or one to be imitated, but a vision of life as hearty and fleeting as laughter and something like the terms by which he lived.

John Cheever, *The Wapshot Chronicle*

It would be worth the while to build still more deliberately than I did, considering, for instance, what foundation a door, a window, a cellar, a garret, have in the nature of man, and perchance never raising any superstructure until we found a better reason for it than our temporal necessities even.

Henry David Thoreau, *Walden*

Introduction

An acquaintance recently watched the moving van pull away from his old house on its way to his new one and had a fleeting thought: "I wouldn't mind if it just kept going and took all that stuff out of my life — except for a few things."

We humans have one instinct to acquire and another to unburden. Call one our material bias and the other our freedom bias. Both are rooted in evolution.

Before civilization ensured year-round plenty, our ancestors layered on fat and stocked up on supplies to get through lean times. It's their blood in our veins that makes us overeat and hold on to junk because we "may need it someday." They vied to impress potential mates by advertising their fitness as providers. Because this was a prerequisite for reproduction, we're bred to seek status in possessions. While this scarcity-based behavior pattern is outmoded, we unconsciously march to its beat. Our inherited insatiability no longer serves survival of the species but endangers the planet. If not for our innate compulsion to competitively build and display shelter, the typical home might be what's now considered a small house, under a thousand square feet or so, fitting today's smaller households.

No sooner did we bury ourselves in protection from the elements than we fled back to our first home in the space and freedom of the outdoors, building minimal weekend and summer getaways or camping out to escape the claustrophobia of over-accumulated architecture and belongings. Nature molded us before we bulwarked ourselves against it — first with clothes, then buildings, then cities — and it's still our best-fitting environment. No interior is more pleasing than a natural outdoor setting in good weather; Central Park is the toast of Manhattan.

Instinctively linking shelter to survival, status, and procreation, the materially biased idea of home is wrapped up in ego, insecurity, and fear of death or the extinction of one's line. People still equate their worth and identity with possessions and value an impressive home as a hedge against mortality. From architecture's inception, its power has been abused to claim god-like immortality or authority. Visiting Versailles, it's hard *not* to believe the French monarchy ruled by God's will.

For all this, the commonest critique of overreaching houses has always been that they are less protectors of life than tombs. They not only distance us from nature with their materiality, but squander our time and energy on their response to anxieties about the future, robbing life of immediacy, lightness, and joy. A home that honors our freedom bias would place us in the here and now, redirect our attention from our own mortality to life's wonder, take us out of ourselves, and buoy us with a sense of belonging to humanity at large and nature's timeless scheme.

Edgar Allan Poe's 1841 story, "A Descent into the Maelström," is a parable of missing out on life by clinging to it. Two brothers on a sailboat are slowly spiraling down a giant whirlpool, a metaphor for life's inexorable end. The brother who will survive narrates:

> Having made up my mind to hope no more, I got rid of a great deal of that terror which unmanned me at first…. I began to reflect how magnificent it was to die in such a manner, and how foolish it was in me to think of so paltry a consideration as my own individual life, in view of so wonderful a manifestation of God's power…. After a little while I became possessed with the keenest curiosity about the whirl itself. I positively felt a wish to explore its depths, even at the sacrifice I was going to make; and my principal grief was that I should never be able to tell my old companions on shore about the mysteries I should see.

His calm allows him to observe how the boat and other large objects descend into the whirlpool faster than smaller debris. Clearly, their best chance of survival is to abandon ship. He tries to tell his brother, frozen in terror and clinging to a deck bolt he has just commandeered from the narrator, "a raving maniac through sheer fright" sadly succumbing to his instinct for self-preservation. The brother mistakes the greatest material attachment for security, blinded to opportunity by his mortal fear. Unable to pry him away, the narrator lashes himself to a barrel and throws himself overboard. Boat and brother are pulled under while the narrator lives to see the whirlpool subside. His survival is a matter of symbolism and providing the tale a living narrator; even if he had died, his last moments would have been far richer than his brother's and a highlight of his own life.

This theme of living more vitally through material rejection and communion with nature is most insightfully explored in Henry David Thoreau's *Walden*. The enduring appeal of Thoreau's call for redemptive simplicity underlies the popular fascination with small prefab and tiny houses, the epic sales of Marie Kondo's *Life-Changing Magic of Tidying Up*, and the market dominance of Apple's minimalist design ethos.

A parallel reductive current has flowed through the history of architectural theory and practice. Marc-Antoine Laugier's *Essay on Architecture* called for a return to the honest first principles of the primitive hut a century before *Walden* celebrated the authenticity of life in a 150-square-foot cabin. The prevailing minimalism of today's architecture aligns with Thoreau's rejection of all but "life's essentials." While the discipline of architecture has many lessons for anyone who would build a house, they remain largely unshared because of the chasm between the profession and the common person. Few people live in a house designed to order by an architect, but the profession could teach us how to make homes that exploit our freedom bias and keep our material bias from exploiting *us*.

The divide between architecture and ordinary people struck me some years ago when a young couple asked my opinion, as an architect, of a design in a house-plan book. Like most such designs today, it prioritized capacity, convenience, and curb appeal. I disliked it, but couldn't pinpoint any single glaring flaw. The house had functionally related rooms and a typical suburban street façade, but aspired to little else. It felt like a missed opportunity. The interior was constrained within an exterior of forced complexity motivated above all by avoidance of simplicity which, apparently, might suggest poverty. The design gave no hint that Frank Lloyd Wright or any other great pioneer of home design had ever changed the way architects think about houses.

A copy of the architectural historian James S. Ackerman's book, *Palladio*, was at hand, and soon I was showing the couple how much their plan differed from the Renaissance architect's villas. They were entitled to their bewilderment; Palladio's grand classical buildings sprouted statues of Roman gods but lacked indoor plumbing. In fact, most weren't primary homes at all but country retreats, pleasure palaces built for the leisure of noblemen with servants to cushion any architectural impracticality. It would have appeared just as pointless to show them iconic modern houses. Mies van der Rohe's mid-twentieth-century Farnsworth House was a ridiculously expensive one-room glass box for a privileged client who notoriously found it impractical even as a weekend house (although Mies's advocate Philip Johnson was so impressed by it he built a version for himself.)

Among Palladio's designs was the Villa Rotonda, a truly fundamental act of architecture. In contrast to the indifferent jumble of today's typical house, it has focus, informing ideas, grandeur, deep human resonance, and an ordering hierarchy of spaces building to a climax, all things even a small house can aspire to. The villa was first published in Palladio's *Four Books of Architecture*, the profession's most influential how-to book, which Thomas Jefferson called his design "bible." What did it say that our discussion had led here? I was introducing my listeners to the basics of architectural thought. It occurred to me that there was no putting a finger on precisely what was wrong with their house plan because it simply lacked everything an architectural education has to offer.

On the surface, neither the monumental Villa Rotonda nor the fishbowl Farnsworth House is a practical model for most people, but they operate on multiple levels holding invaluable lessons even for those on a budget. For one, their prioritization of pleasure makes them worth studying by anyone who would design a joyful house. Vitruvius asserted two thousand years ago that "Well building hath three conditions: commodity, firmness and delight," in Sir Henry Wotton's venerable translation. Although country houses and weekend retreats are second homes, they have always been on the cutting edge of house design because delight is their first order of business. In his book, *The Villa*, Ackerman explains:

Created as the Renaissance sought inspiration in the ancient past, Andrea Palladio's Villa Rotonda (1566–1606) was based on his misconception that antiquity's vanished houses must have resembled its surviving temples.

> A villa is a building in the country designed for its owner's enjoyment and relaxation. Though it may also be the center of an agricultural enterprise, the pleasure factor is what essentially distinguishes the villa residence from the farmhouse and the villa estate from the farm. The farmhouse tends to be simple in structure and to conserve ancient forms that do not require the intervention of a designer. The villa is typically the product of an architect's imagination and asserts its modernity. The basic program of the villa has remained unchanged for more than two thousand years since it was first fixed by the patricians of ancient Rome.

Ackerman notes that this constancy of purpose is unique to the villa. Other building types have evolved in response to new conditions and demands,

> but the villa has remained substantially the same because it fills a need that never alters, a need which, because it is not material but psychological and ideological, is not subject to the influences of evolving societies and technologies. The villa accommodates a fantasy which is impervious to reality.

Modern villas like the Farnsworth House and Philip Johnson's Glass House argue that this fantasy is best pursued with open, one-room houses that embrace nature. (After all, the richest patrician can only be in one room at a time.) Evoking

The processional steps ascending to Mies van der Rohe's single-room Farnsworth House (1946–1951) enhance its temple aura.

Philip Johnson's earthbound Glass House (1947–1949) conjoins the temple's one-room character with that of the primitive hut, an archetype idealized as the work of early man still part and parcel of nature.

the lightness we once enjoyed in nature, they embody the ideal of a small, simple, undemanding retreat in the spirit of Thoreau's cabin.

Can the lessons and spirit of *any* villa with verdant 360-degree views be applied to full-time homes in affordable, working-class neighborhoods? Ackerman states that the villa can only be understood as a satellite of and refuge from its owner's city house. The villa gives calm pleasure in rural nature, far from the messy urban realm of work, commerce, and the madding crowd. The modern suburb, conceived to marry country pleasure with daily access to city work under one roof, has only resulted in soul-deadening and unsustainable sprawl. Denser, walkable communities of smaller houses are more environmentally and socially beneficial, but even farther from the traditional villa setting. To emulate a villa, such houses would need to adapt to the reality of their site, balancing greater demands for privacy with exposure to the natural world. They would also need to exploit every opportunity to simulate the preferred outdoor environment of our first ancestors, who live on in us.

The likes and dislikes of our primitive forebears, forged in life-and-death situations, are deeply ingrained in us. Protective traits, like an alertness to snakes, helped them survive to reproduce and perpetuate such attributes through generations. Much of our response to both natural and built surroundings is thus involuntary, bodily, and shaped by our species' past. The pronounced effect on our mood of sunny or rainy days, of the first hint of spring or fall in the air, are vestiges of a once more consequential relation to the environment. Atmospheric conditions retain an outsize hold on us.

Light is nature's essential transforming element, both externally and, as twilight's magic tells us, psychologically. Optimizing it can make a home a natural retreat regardless of its setting. Small houses with fewer rooms have a built-in advantage for light. A one-room-deep house, for example, can admit light to the same space from front and back, simulating its ambient outdoor quality. As it refreshes our surroundings, changing light puts us in the moment, sharpens our senses, and renews our wonder at life. This occurs dramatically when we're transfixed by a storm that would have more justifiably riveted our forebears at nature's mercy. Anthony Hecht captures the effect in his poem "Apprehensions," whose narrator recounts his boyhood experience of an approaching storm:

I, at the window, studiously watching
A marvelous transformation of the sky;
A storm was coming up by dark gradations.
But what was curious about this was
That as the sky seemed to be taking on
An ashy blankness, behind which there lay
Tonalities of lilac and dusty rose
Tarnishing now to something more than dusk,
Crepuscular and funerary greys,
The streets became more luminous, the world
Glinted and shone with an uncanny freshness.
The brickwork of the house across the street
(A grim, run-down Victorian chateau)
Became distinct and legible; the air,
Full of excited imminence, stood still.
The streetcar tracks gleamed like the path of snails.
And all of this made me superbly happy,
But most of all a yellow Checker Cab
Parked at the corner. Something in the light
Was making this the yellowest thing on earth.
It was as if Adam, having completed
Naming the animals, had started in
On colors, and had found his primary pigment
Here, in a taxi cab, on Eighty-ninth Street.
It was the absolute, parental yellow.
Trash littered the gutter, the chipped paint
Of the lamppost still was chipped, but everything
Seemed meant to be as it was, seemed so designed,
As if the world had just then been created,
Not as a garden, but a rather soiled,
Loud, urban intersection, by God's will.

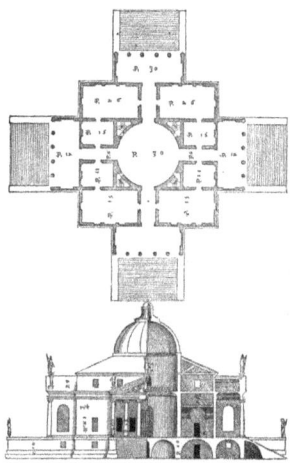

The engraving of the Villa Rotonda in Palladio's *Four Books of Architecture* (1570) is one of architecture's most renowned images.

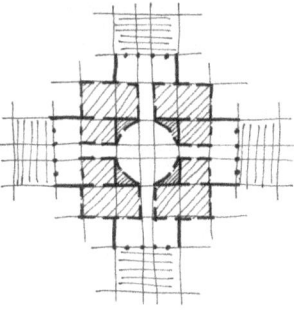

A grid pattern comprehensively lays out the Villa Rotonda's floor plan. The clear primacy of the central space lends the plan to a one-room reading.

The landscapes our forebears navigated have left their impression on our minds. Like light, they are a universal resource from which to create a more rewardingly natural house anywhere. Here again, the Villa Rotonda is an inspiration. Its very grandeur evokes that of nature. Completing a gentle hilltop, it is *of* the landscape. Primitive man, who was both hunter and hunted, would have prized its strategic command of the terrain. The villa's central rotunda, though ringed by other rooms, has views of the landscape on every side when exterior doors are open. Its height reaches for that of outdoor space. Vincenzo Scamozzi, who completed the villa after Palladio's death, planned to give it an oculus like Rome's Pantheon, actually exposing the sky. Walking outside between the tree-like columns of its porticos reenacts our early ancestors' emergence from the shelter of the forest. The visceral reaction buildings can evoke in us comes of such echoes. Great architecture resonates with the depth of past lives inside us, revealing a profound inner dimension.

The Villa Rotonda is instructive in other ways. Its plan is generated from a grid diagram which establishes all at once its circulation spaces and a practical mix of large and small rooms, each pure in itself while fitting perfectly with the others into a compact, unified whole. This diagram also allows for alignment of doorways and windows among the rooms, ensuring clear sightlines through the entire house to surrounding nature. The grid extends outdoors, guiding placement of the porches and exterior stairs, leading the inner order and the eye into the landscape, and so blending inside and out. While the villa's four temple-front façades and rotunda are extravagant, its economical square footprint offsets their cost.

In plan, the roughly triangular masses at the central rotunda's "corners" contain four stairs. They fall within what can be considered thickened walls, a masked service zone architects call *poché*, after the French for the shading that indicates cut-through walls on floor plans. Palladio merged the stairs' circulatory support with the substance and structural support of walls, satisfying the human desire for simplicity by implying a black-and-white plan made only of geometrically pure spaces and solid matter.

From here it's easy to see the villa's outer ring of rooms as cavities carved from very thick walls separating the rotunda from the outdoors. This gives the villa the unified spirit of one of architecture's most powerful archetypes, the one-room building. It was named for the most famous of these, the Pantheon, then used as a church called Santa Maria Rotonda. The villa is often simply called "La Rotonda" as if it had no other spaces. Here again we see architecture's reductive tendency. While hardly a primitive hut, in fronting on every direction the villa suggests another small-house touchstone — the one-space, open-sided pavilion. Modern residential icons like the Farnsworth House adopt the pavilion ideal for its internal and external clarity, access to nature on all sides, and garden-tent associations of pleasure.

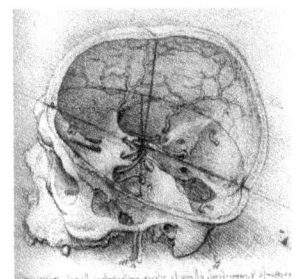

Leonardo da Vinci's drawing of a skull (c. 1489) suggests the notion of the body as a single-chambered temple of the soul.

On yet another level, Palladio's villa resonates with our human identity. Its defining rotunda is a single heart under a domed head, recalling sketches superimposing the human body on buildings by the Renaissance architect Francesco di Giorgio Martini, who espoused an architecture relatably modeled on the body. This is far from an esthete's fantasy. From the moment our mothers imprint the human form on our infant consciousness, we find it everywhere. We can't help seeing a face in a car front, in a door between two windows, even in a two-keystroke emoji. Small houses are cozy because their scale, closer to that of our bodies, makes them feel more human.

Nicolas Beatrizet's engraving of the Pantheon (1553) applies da Vinci's cutaway technique to a one-room temple.

We especially identify with the unity of one-room buildings, from tepees to temples, because their one-to-one relationship of container to contained mirrors that of body to spirit. In his influential 1946 essay, "Heavenly Mansions: An Interpretation of Gothic," Sir John Summerson noted that the statue of the deity in a temple is often covered by a four-posted canopy, its own exclusive mini-temple. This shrine is called an *aedicula*, Latin for "little building." Summerson sees this form in Pompeian wall paintings and observes that it

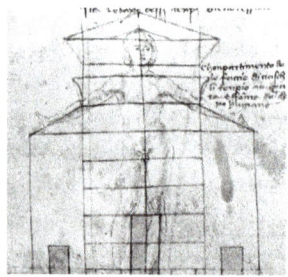

An Illustration from Francesco di Giorgio Martini's first *Treatise on Architecture* (c. 1475–80) overlays the human body on the façade of a church.

The entrance of an otherwise restrained Georgian house concentrates design energy into a person-sized representation of home where all who enter momentarily stand.

"was woven into the development of architecture — both temple architecture and domestic architecture." He points out that entire Gothic cathedrals are piled-up individual shrines, "heavenly mansions," formed by countless pointed arches often housing a statuary figure and always representing a singular spirit. In the elaborate, aedicular front-door frames of Georgian houses he finds a symbol of shelter fitted to the scale of the individual. Aediculae represent the ideal of a refuge close-fitting enough to avoid admitting too much of the outside world. Summerson related the ceremonial quality of the shrine to the private nature of the play houses children improvise under tables — "the idea of neatness and serenity within, contrasting with wildness and confusion without." He observed: "The concept of the diminutive in building exercises a most powerful fascination. The 'little house' is a phrase which goes straight to the heart, whereas 'the big house' is reserved for the prison and the public assistance institution."

Summerson is hardly the first to draw a lesson from children's unschooled preferences. The joy of childhood's pre-civilized naturalness corresponds to the mythic Golden Age before man's fall — Kenneth Grahame even titled his book celebrating childhood wonder *The Golden Age*. The child's play house correlates with the mythic Primitive Hut which has long haunted the imagination of architects and theorists — innocent early man's first home, championed as "*right* because it was *first*" according to Joseph Rykwert in his study, *On Adam's House in Paradise: The Idea of the Primitive Hut in Architectural History*. Whether originating in the early age of the individual or the human race, the vision of a lost paradise involves a small house. The home that captures its spirit promises renewal to adults who've forgotten what it is to be young.

Economic necessity is neither the only nor the best reason to build a small home. It suggests a damage-control design approach aimed at making limited space feel less cramped. It would be a sadly missed opportunity not to also make the most of the many ways only a little house can go to the heart, to embrace smallness as its own thrilling reward the way a sports car does, to build a home that never needs to be escaped because it *is* the escape. Exploring how these and other points can inform the design of a small home, the following fifty short chapters are interspersed with four example houses putting them into practice.

How to Design a Small House

1 | Demographics

The U.S. Census Bureau reports that from 1970 to 2012 the share of households made up of a married couple with children under eighteen fell from 40% to just 20%, the proportion of one-person households increased from 17% to 27%, and the average number of people per household fell from 3.1 to 2.6.

Over the same period, the share of one- and two-bedroom homes in new house construction fell from about 50% to about 30%, while the share of three- and four-bedroom houses rose from about 50% to about 70%, creating a glut of empty bedrooms. Paradoxically, 55% of households are now made up of either an individual or a couple who might be served by a one- or two-bedroom home. Area per person of new houses has quadrupled in the last century.

Flying in the face of steadily shrinking households, the average American house has grown from about 1,000 square feet in 1950 to about 1,500 in 1970 to about 2,500 today. Forces beyond need are clearly responsible. These include status seeking, the profit motives of developers, and fear that smaller houses will have limited resale value despite evidence of ever-smaller households.

Ironically, while the size of houses has increased in the United States, and especially on a per capita basis, surveys show the overall level of happiness of the population has not risen in the past quarter century, and in fact may have declined.

James D. Lutz, *Lest We Forget: A Short History of Housing in the United States*

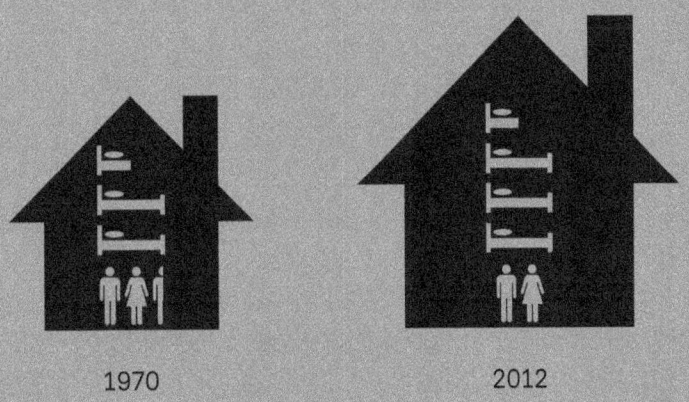

1970   2012

2 | Architects

Only a tiny percentage of homes are designed specifically for their owners by architects. These are a separate species from the typical development house. They may be published or even help shape architectural history. Architects hired to design tract houses tend to be anonymous, service-oriented practitioners willing to work within predictably profitable design formulas. Their client is not the homeowner but a risk-averse developer fearful of creativity and clinging for dear life to the tried and true. Because developers pander to the home buyer's presumed conformity, insecurity, and materialism, their products are bland, pretentious, or both.

    Architecture books surveying iconic modern houses proceed within the first half of the twentieth century from craggy mansions with servant and guest rooms to sleek, sometimes one-room, minimalist glass boxes. Conversely, the typical home of everyman has gone from compact foursquare colonial or Cape Cod to faux manor bristling with projections and inflated with unused rooms. Modern architecture's exploration of small house potential couldn't be more in tune with today's smaller households, but the architectural profession remains divorced from the common man.

    Building a small house can leave money in the budget for self-financing and the chance to work with an architect on an imaginatively personalized home. To quote architect Tom Kundig: "People who build their own home tend to be very courageous. These people are curious about life. They're thinking about what it means to live in a house, rather than just buying a commodity and making it work."

Charles Rennie Mackintosh's 1903 Hill House and Philip Johnson's 1949 Glass House demonstrate the radical reduction in size and complexity of architecturally significant houses in just forty-six years.

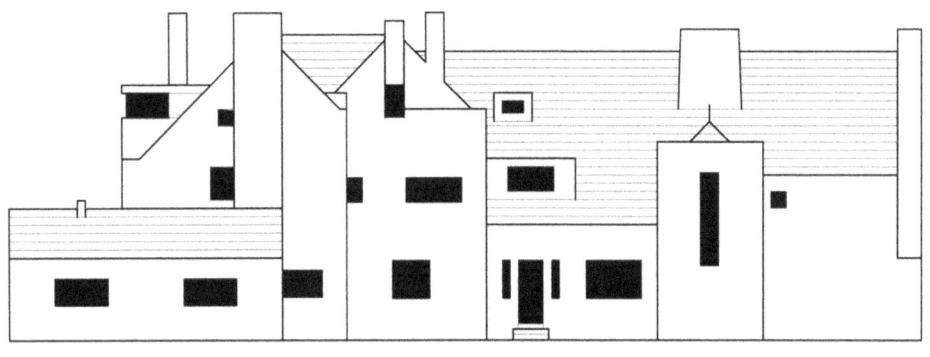

1903

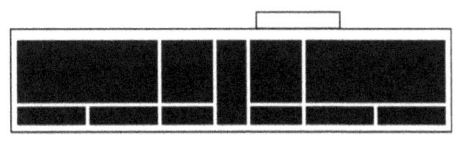

1949

3 | Prefabs

Prefabricated houses are built to high standards with little waste. They bring to construction the assembly-line efficiency of automotive production, a potential which has long tantalized architects. Prefabs may be somewhat more affordable than comparable site-built houses but their real advantage lies in factory-floor quality control.

Truck delivery limits the size of prefabricated house modules. While they can be combined on site into a larger house, their maximum highway-legal dimensions remain a formidable design restriction.

Prefabricated modules need the stiffness to be lifted by crane from a truck bed onto a foundation without buckling. Each one must therefore be a rigid box with integral floor and ceiling or roof. This precludes the efficiency of a poured concrete slab-on-grade floor (Ch. 8). The box's top is redundant with the bottom of any module or separate roof placed above.

Prefabs lend themselves to being set on a foundation rising above ground level over a crawl space or basement, either of which carries its own complicating code requirements. This elevating of the main floor also works against wheelchair accessibility and indoor-outdoor flow.

Trees may have to be cleared for prefab modules to be swung into place, adding cost and potentially reducing site appeal.

While modular houses can be customized, the final product may still not be as adapted to the owner's preferences or the site's unique limitations and opportunities as a fully custom, site-built house. Unlike cars, which are designed for all settings, a house has only one to make the most of.

Houses must go up all of a piece, made by machine tools in a factory, assembled as Ford assembles cars, on moving conveyor belts.

Le Corbusier

If cars were being designed at the rate of architecture we'd still be driving wooden cars.

Bruce Mau

The prefabricated house is inevitable, and a good thing.

Frank Lloyd Wright

Walter Gropius came to see me at my house at Canoas above Rio. I designed it in a sequence of natural curves to flow in and out of the existing landscape. He said, it's beautiful, but it can't be mass-produced. As if I had intended such a thing! What an idiot.

Oscar Niemeyer

4 | Tiny Houses

Tiny houses are typically on wheels and 400 square feet or smaller. Regulated much like recreational vehicles, they fly under the more substantial construction code and zoning requirements for permanently sited houses. They are akin to house trailers, but with more house-like construction and appearance, and often custom built. The tiny house movement is fueled partly by desperation over wage stagnation in the face of ballooning housing costs, the kind of affordability gap that's always underpinned the trailer industry. But the movement also concerns rejection of materialism and voluntary pursuit of a minimalist lifestyle.

While the severe dimensional constraints and raised floors of tiny houses work against many of this book's ideas, Thoreau's Walden is a shared point of reference. The writer built his one-room cabin at Walden Pond, the prototypical tiny house, to confront for once life's essentials, the worthiest of reasons. But Thoreau stayed only two years, two months, and two days, never making a case for a permanent mini-home. Nonetheless, popular interest in the tiny house movement, where design firms and models named Walden abound, tells us how vital his thinking remains.

Tiny houses have gained credibility in recent years. Some cities have changed zoning to allow them, if only as accessory dwelling units to permanent homes, and the 2018 International Residential Code added an appendix specifically covering them. They are the spearhead of an overdue change in attitude toward dwelling and a welcome grassroots challenge to overblown development houses.

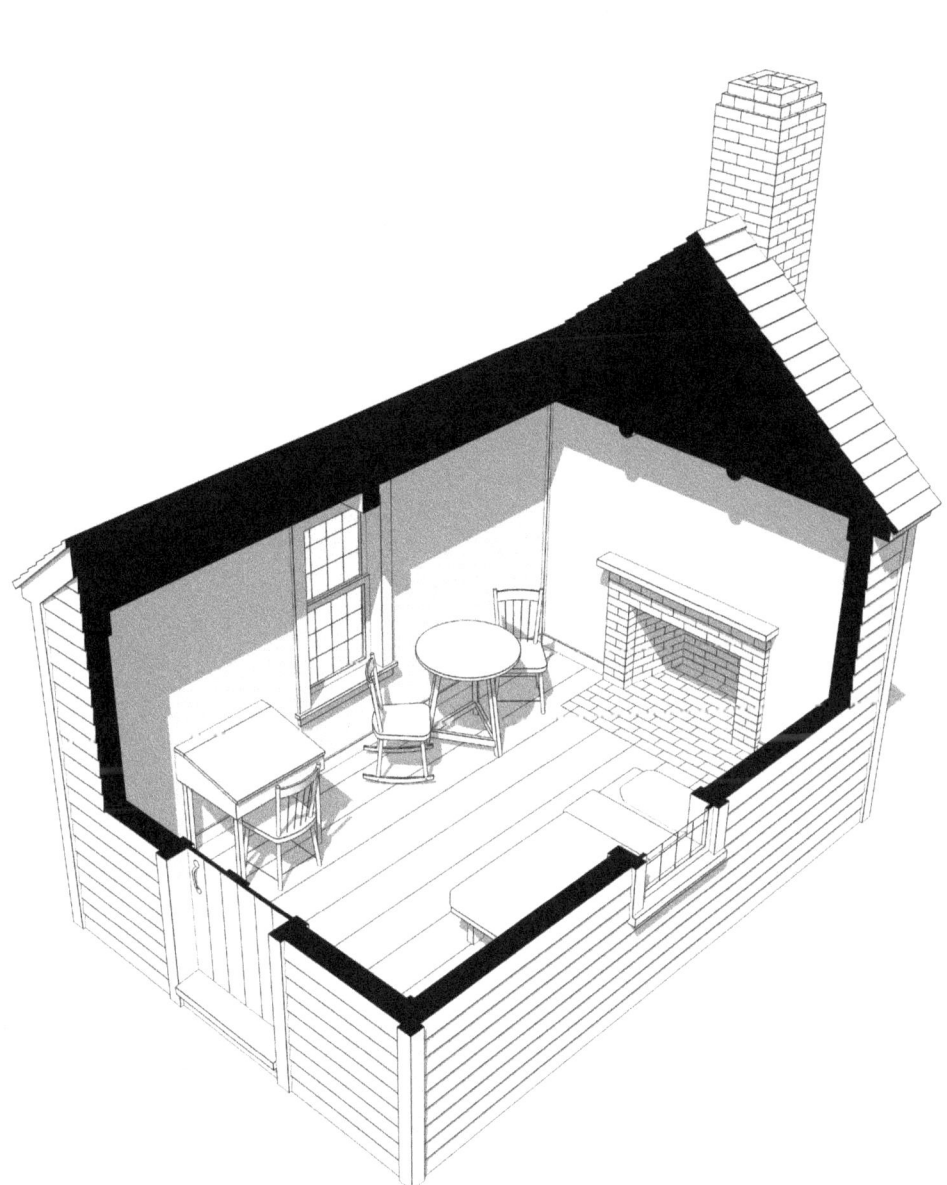

Thoreau's ten-by-fifteen-foot cabin at Walden Pond is a bit wider than the eight and a half feet most tiny houses are limited to by their wheeled chassis. Thoreau's friend Ralph Waldo Emerson let him build on land he owned. Today's tiny-house owners face a greater challenge in finding legal perches. Their search is complicated by the need for electricity and running water, conveniences Thoreau wouldn't have known to miss.

5 | Money

Financing a self-built home is complicated but allows design independence. Banks offering construction loans lack the collateral of a finished home to fall back on, so they impose high down payments and interest rates, especially if the lot isn't already owned. The contractor must pass muster with the bank and funds are released in increments tied to construction stages monitored by the bank. Construction loans typically have a one-year term and then convert to a traditional mortgage.

It's much easier to get a standard mortgage loan for a new house in a development, but this limits the buyer to unimaginative offerings calculated for mass appeal. Developers are reluctant to entertain requests for significant deviations from their standard models, which have safely predictable construction costs and contribute to their idea of a value-enhancing community identity.

Development houses are less about spatial or experiential intangibles than quantities and conveniences easily marketed in advertising shorthand: square footage, bedroom and bathroom counts, master suites, high-end appliance brands, and evocatively named, inauthentic building styles. Developers have a financial interest in selling *more*. Easier financing for their products induces consumers to buy more of what they don't want or need, and spend more of their lives working to pay it off.

The economy of building a small house on a modest lot can enable the alternative of cash funding or a construction loan, allowing both design freedom and the free time that comes with less debt.

Work and consume, an infernal circle . . . in which life's sublime beauty is ignored.

Charlotte Perriand

. . . the insane, sick, dangerous and aggressive idea that men must live only to work and must work to produce and then consume.

Ettore Sottsass

None of the activity stolen by work can be regained by submitting to what work has produced.

Guy Debord

6 | Site

A cabin in nature with no other house in sight is a compelling fantasy. Its high cost prevents most of us from ever learning whether it delivers contentment or boredom and loneliness. A small-house dream is more viable if it trades a wilderness setting for optimized access to trees, sky, and natural light, which can be made available anywhere, in a community that suits our inherently social nature.

Cities and towns are excellent places for small houses, with their affordably compact lots, ready infrastructure, lack of suburban-values zoning, and intrinsic sustainability. They are also more likely to allow car-free living, or at least provide on-street parking. Sidewalks and an interesting mix of zoning uses and public amenities make them more walkable. They're easier places to get to know neighbors.

Cottage communities strung along recreational waterfronts also sometimes offer small lots and infrastructure, together with views.

Pocket neighborhoods are another alternative to anonymous housing tracts or rural isolation. Typically a small cluster of houses — limited to a socially cohesive dozen or so — around a shared outdoor space, they can be initiated by groups of like-minded founders. Parking is usually concentrated at a remove, with houses fronting a companionable green commons instead of the usual paved domain of the car.

Areas of Detroit have streets, sidewalks, water, sewers, and mature trees, just waiting for a new crop of homes.

7 | Footprint

The smaller a house, the less likely anything but a rectangular footprint makes sense. Adding to the obligatory four exterior corners increases construction costs from foundation to roof and makes for a less material- and energy-efficient house which is likely to require more maintenance.

    A large house can successfully employ an irregular plan to embrace and engage outdoor space. As house size falls, this potential diminishes until funds are more rewardingly spent within a simple rectangular shell on higher ceilings, bigger windows, or more square footage. The inefficient envelopes of tract houses straining to impress with needless ins and outs can't compete with the effortless presence of nobly simple barns or saltbox houses.

    A rectangular footprint is easily subdivided into purely shaped spaces and support functions, as in the English two-room cottage plan imported to Colonial America. Its central service zone absorbed a compact entry space, a winding stair, and back-to-back fireplaces. This left cleanly rectangular rooms on either side: the hall, where cooking and entertaining took place, and the more private family parlor. Beyond its efficiency, this diagram offered benefits lacking in many of today's houses. The rooms had balanced light, cross ventilation and the spatial release of exterior exposure on three sides; neither room was intrusively entered directly from the other or by the front door, which had a separate if minimal transition space.

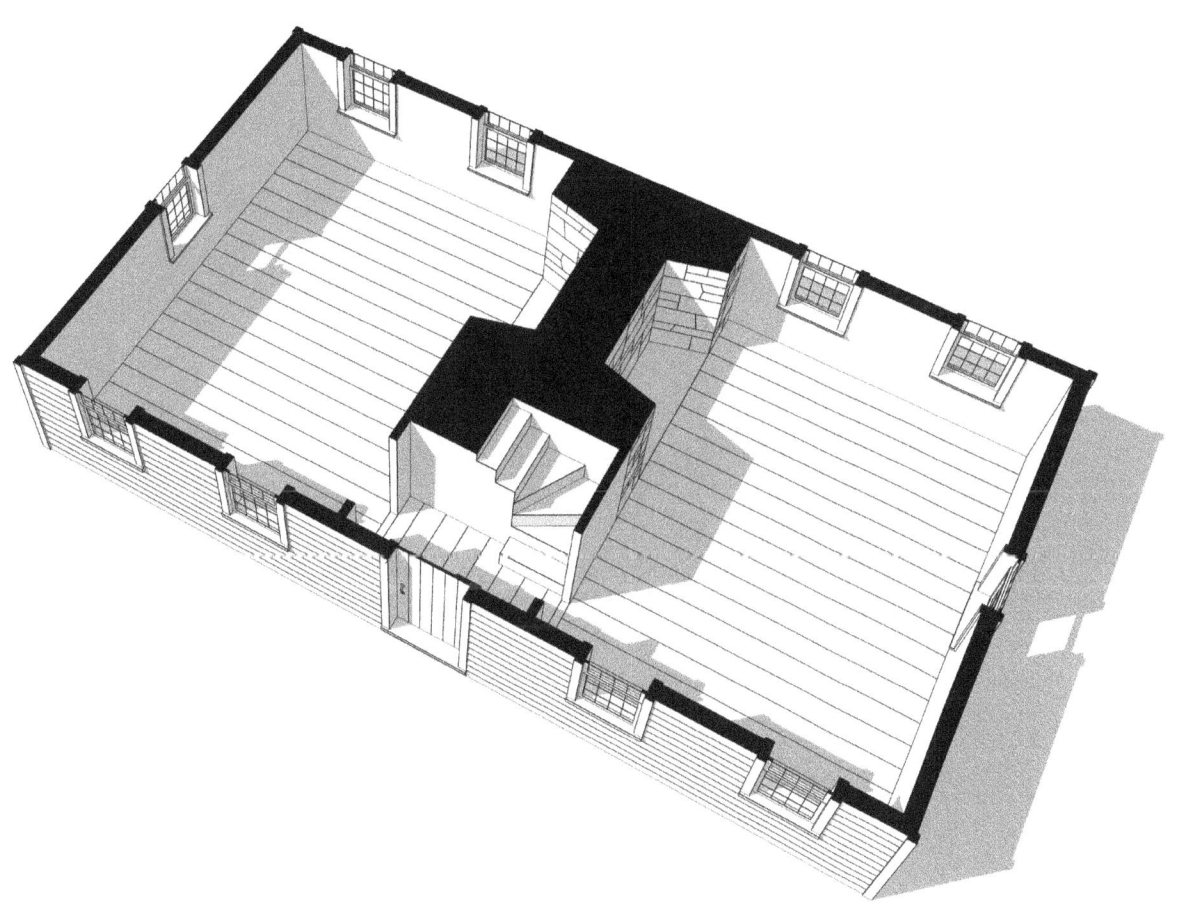

The center-chimney plan of the English two-room cottage was transplanted as the nucleus of early American saltbox, garrison, and Cape Cod houses.

8 | **Stories**

A small house should have one story, for many reasons. Stairs take up the same area in a large or small house but consume a greater percentage of a small one, diluting whatever savings in footprint, foundation, and envelope might come of building a multi-story home. Sleeping and living on separate floors demands multiple bathrooms, a significant consideration given their outsize impact on a house's cost per square foot. Upstairs and downstairs functions rarely require the same area, so one level is usually oversized to match the other. A house with stairs isn't accessible and can't be safely aged into. Freedom from an upstairs encourages a living area with a higher ceiling and taller windows, adding potential for sky exposure, natural light, and views above neighbors. Multiple levels work against the unifying internal clarity and spatial flow that can make a small house worth building.

    A house with no basement or upstairs can be served entirely by a slab-on-grade floor which exploits the bearing capacity of the earth, eliminates the need for a crawlspace or basement, provides an energy-saving thermal mass to reduce temperature swings, and allows efficient, comfortable, radiant-floor heating. This floor places the house at less of a remove from surrounding nature while easing wheelchair access and indoor-outdoor living. Its surface can be polished to a lustrous finish, eliminating the need and expense of applied flooring. A small rectangular house with a slab floor has a garage-like economy to offset the cost of grandeur-imparting features (Ch. 46).

In all but taking the earth for its floor, Erik Gunnar Asplund's Woodland Chapel for the Stockholm Cemetery (1920) achieves a primal power. Inspired by a thatched vernacular cottage Asplund had visited, the Chapel has the comforting simplicity and natural affinity of man's long-idealized first house, the primitive hut.

9 | Accessibility

Their greater potential for one-story design lends small houses to wheelchair accessibility. Slab-on-grade construction facilitates entry via a walk sloped at a wheelchair-friendly grade of 5% or less, or a ramp rising no more than six inches, neither of which requires complicating handrails.

    A house designed to meet the maneuvering-space standards of the Americans with Disabilities Act for accessible routes, bathrooms, and door openings can readily be adapted to full accessibility and with minor modification will accommodate wheelchair-using guests. This can be achieved with a very modest increase in area, especially in a small house with a spacious open plan and minimized corridors.

    Designing a new house for accessibility is much cheaper than retrofitting an existing one. An accessible house sustainably allows for aging in place and has a larger resale market that includes seniors and people with disabilities. Over and above such calculations, accessibility completes a house's humanity.

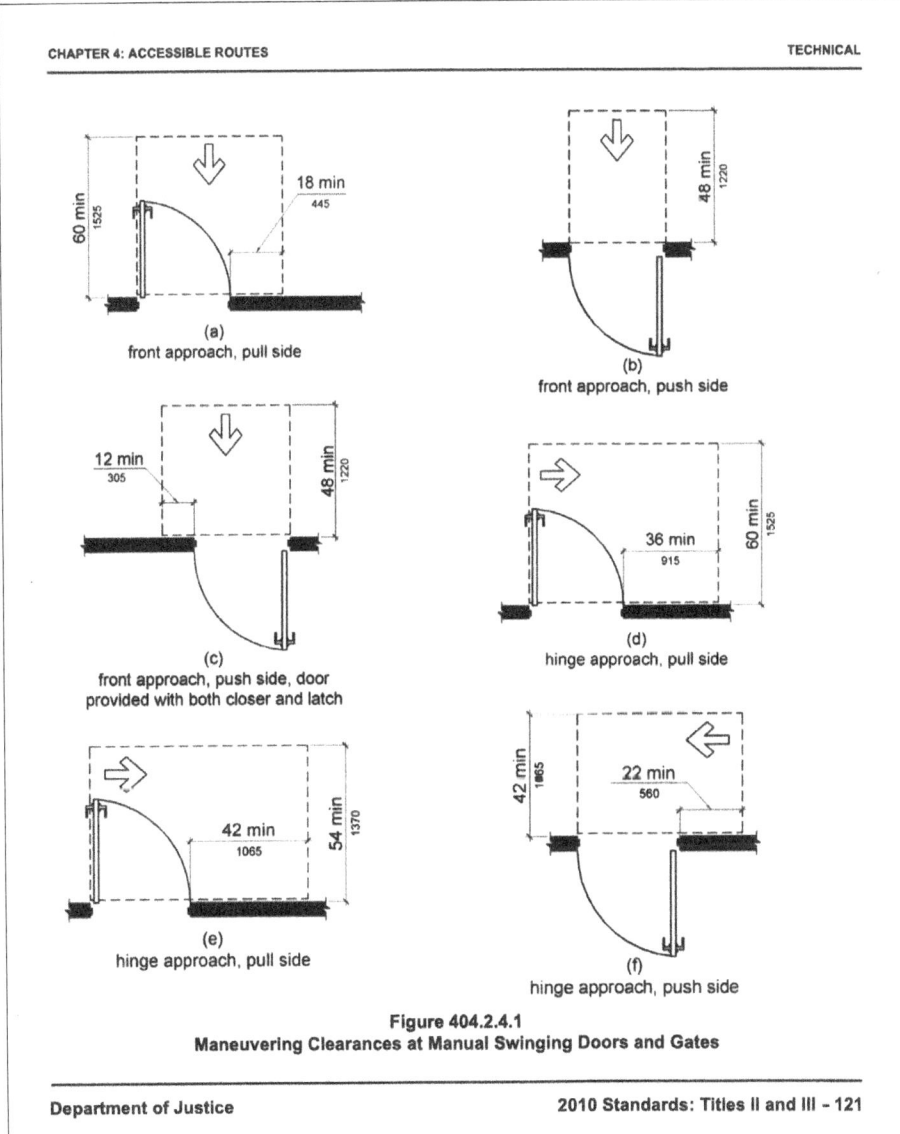

Figure 404.2.4.1
Maneuvering Clearances at Manual Swinging Doors and Gates

Wheelchair maneuvering clearances at doors must be provided in the design of an accessible house. Pocket doors require less space for this than swinging doors in some cases. Their disappearance when open also helps a small house feel less cluttered.

10 | Basement

Basements detract from a small house's appealing simplicity. By code, they must have above-ground escape windows. These typically require the first floor to be raised well above ground and accessed by steps, complicating accessibility, outdoor flow, and house image. Frank Lloyd Wright said of his era's Midwestern houses, "Invariably the damp, sticky clay of the prairie was dug out for a basement under the whole house, and the rubble-stone walls of this dank basement always stuck up above the ground a foot or more and blinked, with half windows."

The first-floor space taken up by a basement-stair opening could instead be used for storage or utilities like a washer and dryer which are often inconveniently relegated to a basement.

A basement collects unneeded things, compromising a small house's special potential for an unencumbered life. It adds a psychologically disturbing, dark, and unseen realm, contradicting our innate desire for openness and clarity (Ch. 40).

Basements are often thought of as free space because they may not contribute to assessed square footage or demand digging much deeper than required by code for foundations to extend below the frost line, but they're no bargain.

A house should — ordinarily — not have a basement. In spite of everything you may do, a basement is a noisome, gaseous damp place. From it come damp atmospheres and unhealthful conditions. Because people rarely go there — and certainly not to live there — it is almost always sure to be an ugly place. The family tendency is to throw things into it, leave them there and forget them. It usually becomes . . . a great, furtive underground for the house in order to enable the occupants to live in it disreputably.

Frank Lloyd Wright, *The Natural House*

Example

40' × 28'
1,120 square feet
12' & 8' ceilings

The generative diagram for this house creates a central service zone containing entry hall, bathroom, closets, and short corridors. On one side is a living space with privacy-providing high front windows above a single-galley kitchen (Ch. 44) and a rear glazed wall opening to a terrace through sliding glass doors. The dining table doubles as a brightly daylit kitchen island. Two rooms on the other side of the house can serve as bedrooms or a bedroom and a study. The plan diagram follows the example of the historic two-room, center-chimney house with a service core buffering a more public "hall" side from a more private "parlor" side (Ch. 7). A system of pocket doors in the central zone allows the entry hall, front bedroom/study, and toilet to be sealed off from the rest of the house, creating a home-office suite that can accommodate business visitors in privacy from the rest of the house (Ch. 16). Multiple bathroom doors allow a near elimination of corridors. The living space has sightlines through windows in the smaller rooms for spatial release. These windows create opportunities for daylit work spaces at a quiet remove from the living area.

Example A
Plan

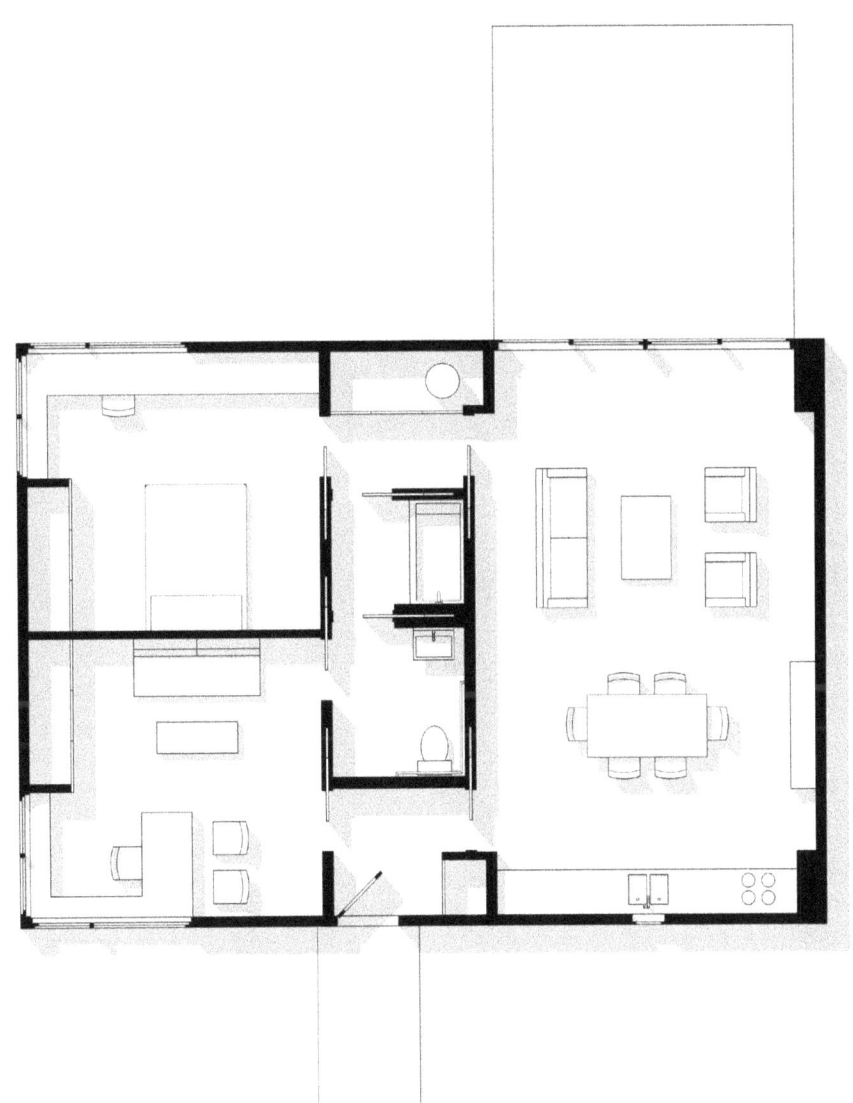

Example A
Low plan perspective from front

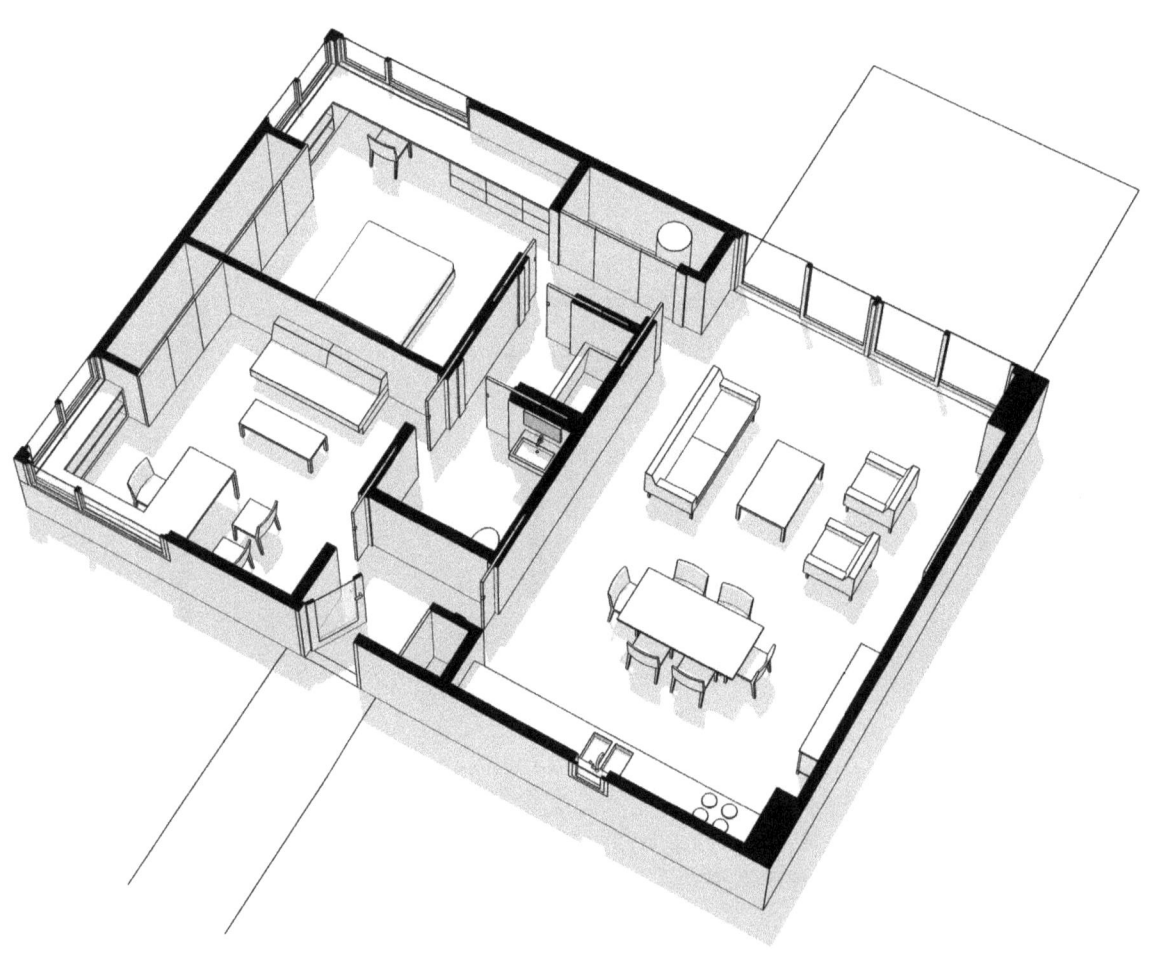

Example A
High plan perspective from rear

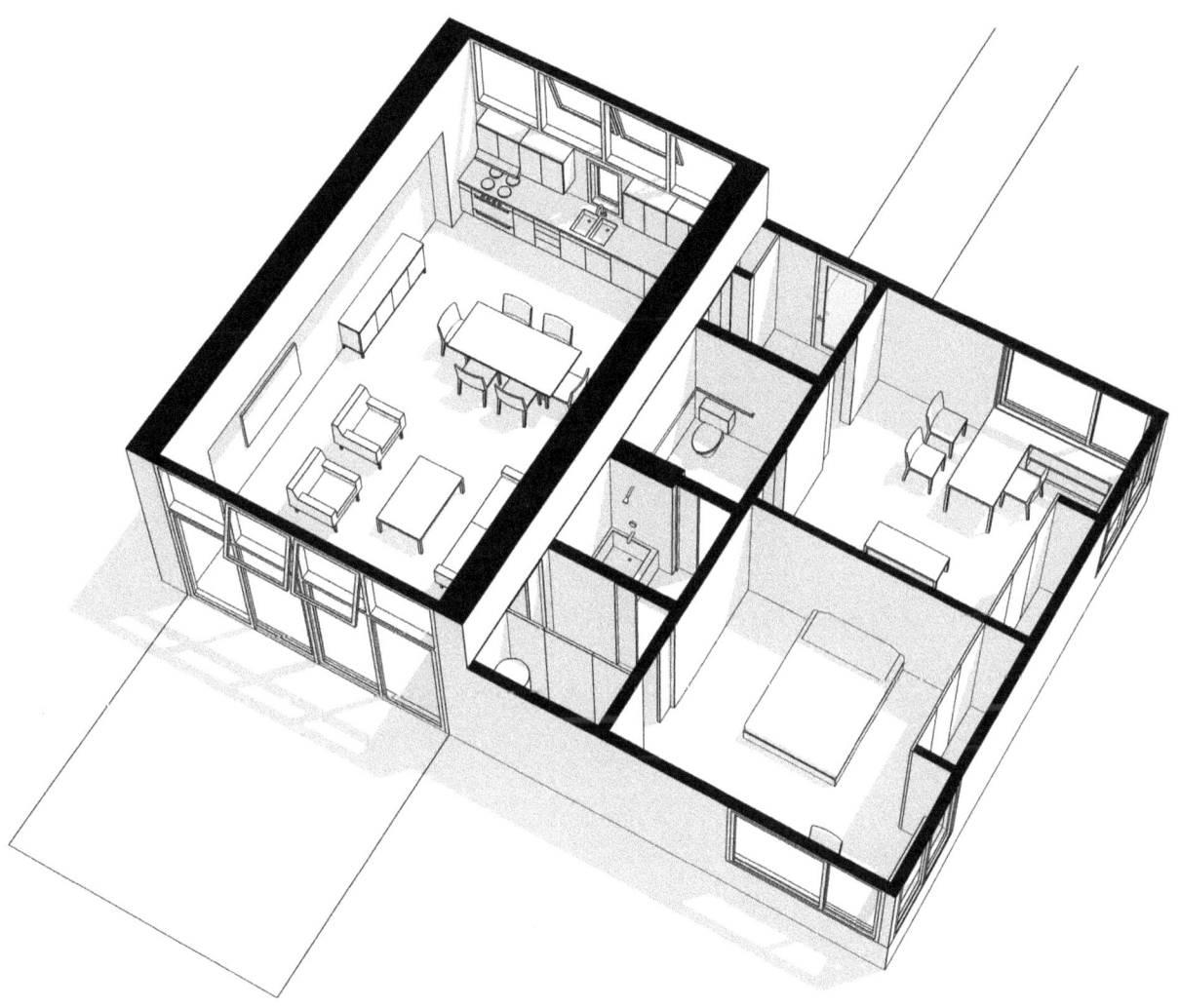

Example A
Front

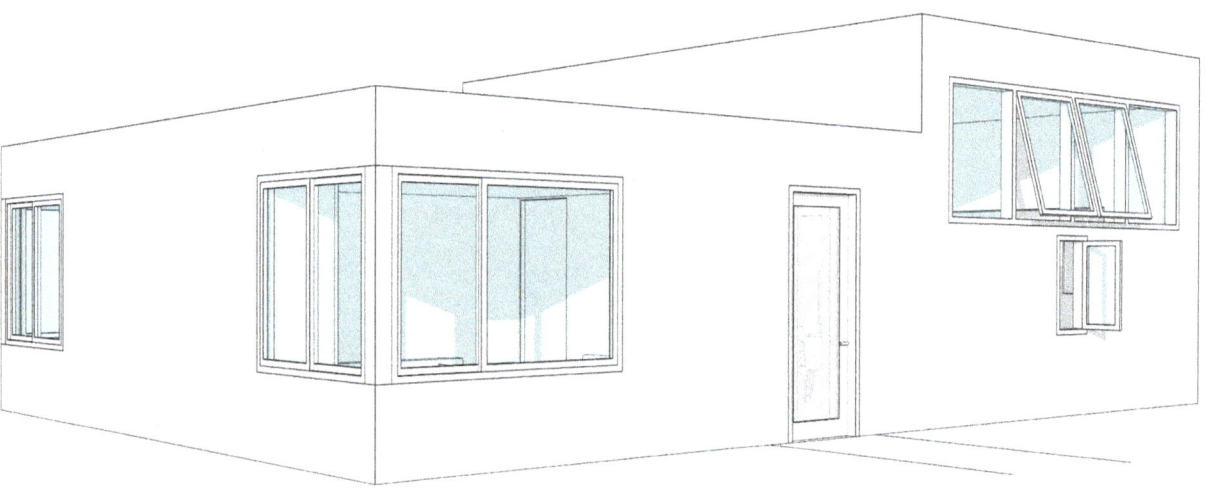

Example A
Rear

Example A
Top: Section key plan
Bottom: Section B-B

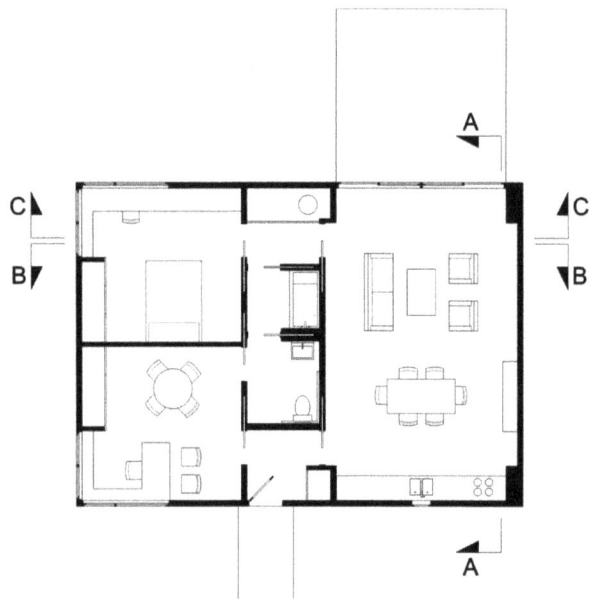

Example A
Top: Section A-A
Bottom: Section C-C

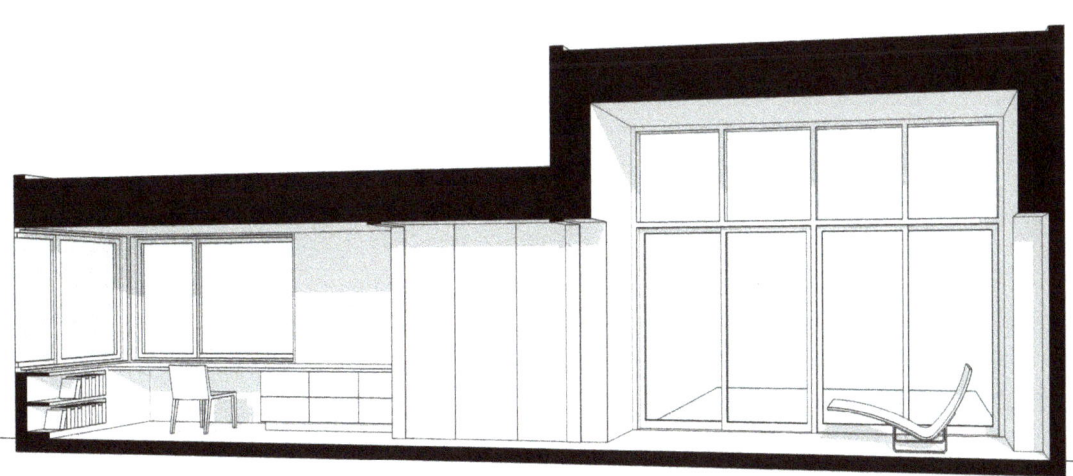

11 | Garage

On-demand driverless cars may soon make garages and driveways obsolete. This would allow smaller house lots and less pavement, enhancing sustainability and affordability. An attached garage demeans any house but especially a small one, of which it is a greater part, making it seem as much a home for cars as humans.

The attached garage has other drawbacks. Its door leading into the house is usually the most commonly used way in, effectively the main entrance, typically turning the kitchen into a de facto entry hall. Guests are made to feel somewhat presumptuous for knocking on the now strictly ceremonial front door. Multiple points of access into a house detract from its aura of private refuge. On a subconscious level, entrances are potential points of sudden intrusion or distraction. Our inherited wariness prefers a single control point.

The garden tools and recreational items typically kept in a garage can instead occupy storage space built into the side of a house with doors opening to the exterior.

Car culture dictates our depressingly banal modern world of expressways, malls, office parks, and homogeneous housing tracts. It steamrolls the magic, mystery, and romance out of life. The pace and scale of traffic and its infrastructure are inhuman. There is nowhere more placeless or negatingly indifferent to man or nature than the edge of a highway. A house gains in its spirit of refuge, humanity, and naturalness with every step it takes from the car and its realm.

Without alleys, garages have moved to the front of the house in America. As a matter of design, the garage in front of the house is a disaster. The gigantic door presents a blank wall to the street. Tarted up with extra moldings or a checkerboard paint job, it can look even worse by drawing more attention to itself. Anyway, it is inescapably the dominant feature of the house's front. And if it takes up a third of the façade, which is often the case, then it disfigures what remains, no matter how elegant. Moreover, when you consider that every house on the street has a similar gaping blank façade, you end up with a degraded street as well as a degraded architecture.

James Howard Kunstler, *The Geography of Nowhere: The Rise and Decline of America's Man-Made Landscape*

12 | Porch

Porches resolve our competing needs for shelter and openness, refuge and prospect, by expanding the sweet-spot threshold between indoors and out. They are also a beloved feature of small towns and pocket neighborhoods for inviting engagement with passersby.

Porches have drawbacks, though. Their roofs rob indoor spaces of natural light and block views of trees and sky. They self-defeatingly put the outdoors at arm's length from a house's interior. A porch complicates a house in a way a tree-canopied terrace, which offers many of the same benefits, doesn't.

While even a paragon of minimalism like the Farnsworth house has a porch (Ch. 13), the Glass House it inspired Philip Johnson to build seems more appealingly self-contained for dispensing with one (Ch. 47). Johnson may have viewed his house as its own porch, a useful small-house strategy; the architectural historian Reyner Banham called it "a detached porch looking out in all directions at the Great Out There." Glenn Murcutt, another architect of celebrated homes inspired by the Farnsworth House, has said, "I have a great desire to make a building which is just a big veranda."

This notion is perfectly realized in Mark Twain's freestanding writer's study. An inspiration for any house with a porch sensibility, it certainly inspired Twain. He created much of his literary output there, calling it "the home of" his 1884 masterpiece, *The Adventures of Huckleberry Finn*. His wife wrote that he "was never so good and lovable" nor "worked with such perfect ease and happiness in his life."

The octagonal porch crowning Mark Twain's house (top) just off the billiard room where he wrote anticipates the study (bottom) built for him by his sister-in-law on her farm, where the writer and his family summered. She hired an associate of his house's architect to design the kindred hilltop study. Windowed all around, it foreshadows modernist glass houses. Twain wrote a friend about its command of "leagues of valleys and city and retreating ranges of distant blue hills," reporting, "it is a cozy nest and just room in it for a sofa, table, and three or four chairs, and when the storms sweep down the remote valley and the lightning flashes behind the hills beyond and the rain beats upon the roof over my head — imagine the luxury of it."

13 | Trees

We have an inherited bond with trees. In his 1982 essay, "The Forest Edge," architect Robert Geddes argued that the place where forest meets grassland

> can be seen both as man's ideal habitat and a mythical image. Consequently, just as man historically enjoyed the forest at the edge of the clearing which has offered him both shelter and openness, so today we enjoy being in architecture which recreates similar spatial conditions: arcades and colonnades, loggias and porches, thresholds, cloisters, courtyards and peristyles—all of which resemble clearings at the edge of the forest.

Merely siting a small house amid trees can achieve much of this effect without the cost or complication of a porch or colonnade. Trees let us see and hear the wind. They attract birds and their songs. Their generations of leaves elicit distinctive moods as seasons change and we sense our place in the natural order.

The presence of trees can give even a house on a small urban lot a vital connection to nature. Their moving shadows on interior surfaces animate a home and evoke our evolutionary forest shelter.

New trees planted around a house should be selected with an eye toward falling limbs and leaves. Slender species with small leaves, dappled shade, eloquent fall color, and interesting winter branch patterns make good neighbors.

Mies van der Rohe's Farnsworth House was sited just north of a black maple tree for summer shade crucial to its glass walls. Like a primitive hut, Mies's minimal house is the next thing to sheltering under a tree.

14 | Living

One of Frank Lloyd Wright's great innovations in house design was the removal of partitions between living functions to combine them into one large space. In typical examples like his Hickox House (1900), the dining room, living room, and library align in one pavilion-like space the length of the house, creating the greatest possible interior prospect. The eye is drawn down the long axis and out through bay windows at either end. "Vista within and vista without," Wright called this strategy. In a compact house, such spatial combination can both create a sense of expansiveness and allow circulation paths around furniture groupings to overlap, saving floor area.

A two-zone diagram keeps the Hickox House's service spaces, including formal and service entrances, from disturbing the purity, primacy, and private refuge of the living pavilion. It may help us understand Wright's design process to see these services as falling within a thickened front wall of a compellingly simple one-room building. Controlled openings allow the service side to drop from the living area's consciousness like a backstage, supporting the one-room impression.

The central living room has a terrace so closely aligned with it that the two seem like halves of a whole, blurring the line between indoors and out. The terrace is our ancestors' daytime home on the plain, the hearth opposite is the campfire where they gathered at night. Harmonizing with our ancient daily rhythm, their axis traverses both space and time.

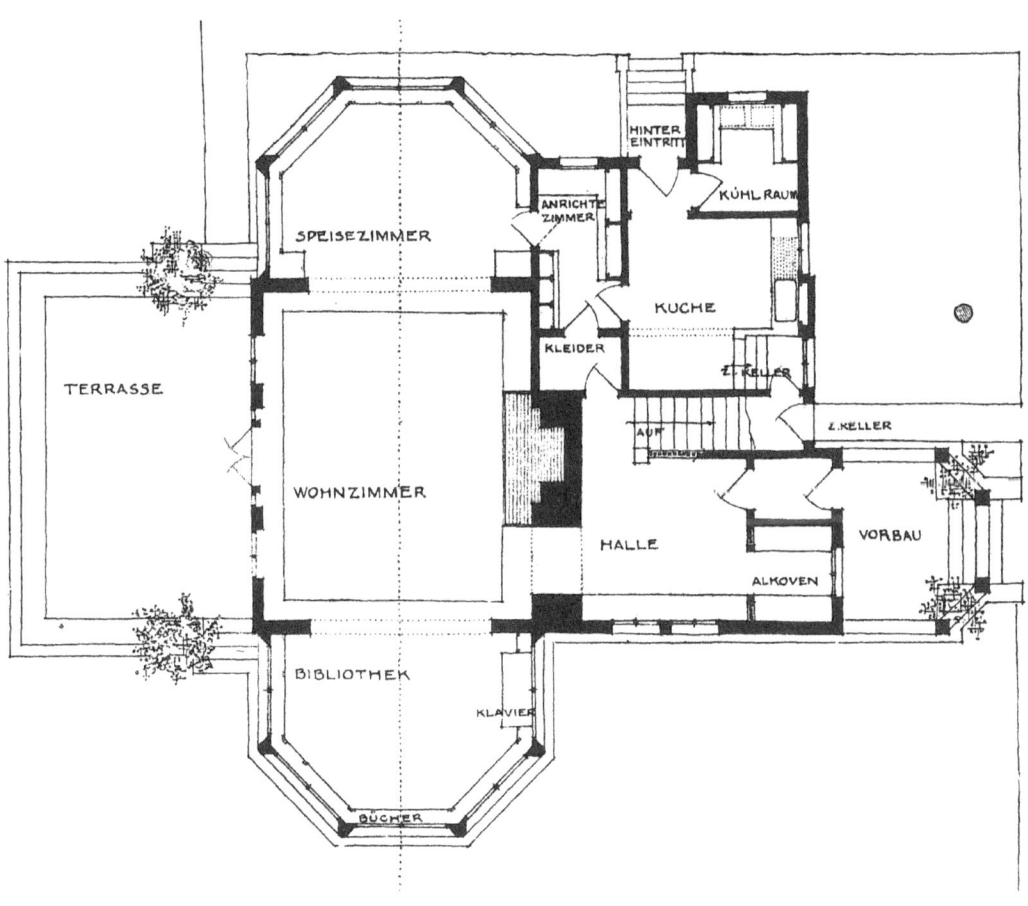

The Hickox House and other Frank Lloyd Wright designs published in the internationally influential 1910 Wasmuth Portfolio of his work changed the course of residential design, paving the way for the one-room Farnsworth House (Ch. 38) and its own proliferating lineage.

15 | Terrace

Terraces, unlike decks or porches, rest on the ground and avoid encumbering steps, crawlspaces, or view-blocking railings.

A terrace should be part of a small house's living space, adjacent to the indoor living area and as open to it as possible, so that one visibly completes the other. This will amplify the interior's volume and association with the outdoors. The closer the living space's floor level to that of the terrace, the greater will be the effect of continuity and the more seamlessly activities will spill outside. A polished-concrete, slab-on-grade floor will most easily align with terrace paving, and the affinity of a concrete floor to stone or concrete terrace pavers will add to their sense of unity. Light, neutral-colored terrace paving will reflect ambient natural light indoors, heightening the interior's outdoor feel without tinting its surfaces. Placing the terrace under tree canopies will enhance its outdoor-room feel, helping identify it with both the indoor living area and our ancestral forest habitat.

A house's generative diagram should include outdoor living, after Frank Lloyd Wright's example. The lines defining his living rooms typically extend outward to room-proportioned terraces or porches, marrying indoors and out (Ch. 14). Even an exception like his early Winslow House fills out a corner of its compact diagram with a terrace that completes the house's symmetry as if it were an actual room (Ch. 43).

A rendering of Frank Lloyd Wright's Cheney House highlights its terrace, which extends the living area outdoors through a window wall with glazed doors. This continuity of indoor and outdoor living space is the core of nearly all of Wright's hundreds of houses.

16 | Entrance

A front door opening directly onto a living area violates a house's sanctuary even when closed, just by its potential to open at any moment. The front door should instead be given a dedicated entryway screened or at least clearly set off from the living area. This is especially important in a small house, with its fewer transitional spaces from public to private.

In snowy climates where an attached garage is deemed necessary and a house will have a secondary entrance from it, this door should be near the primary entrance door and share a dedicated entry space with it. This will consolidate the house's perceived points of intrusion into one, strengthening a domestic sense of private refuge by reassuring our protective instincts.

A house's entrance should be near the kitchen for easy unloading of groceries. This will also allow a host preparing meals for expected guests to easily welcome them.

If a house has a second bedroom that might serve as a home office, the entryway should be located between it and the living area. An entrance space with doors allowing it to mimic an airlock between office and living sides can admit business visitors while respecting the privacy of the rest of the house.

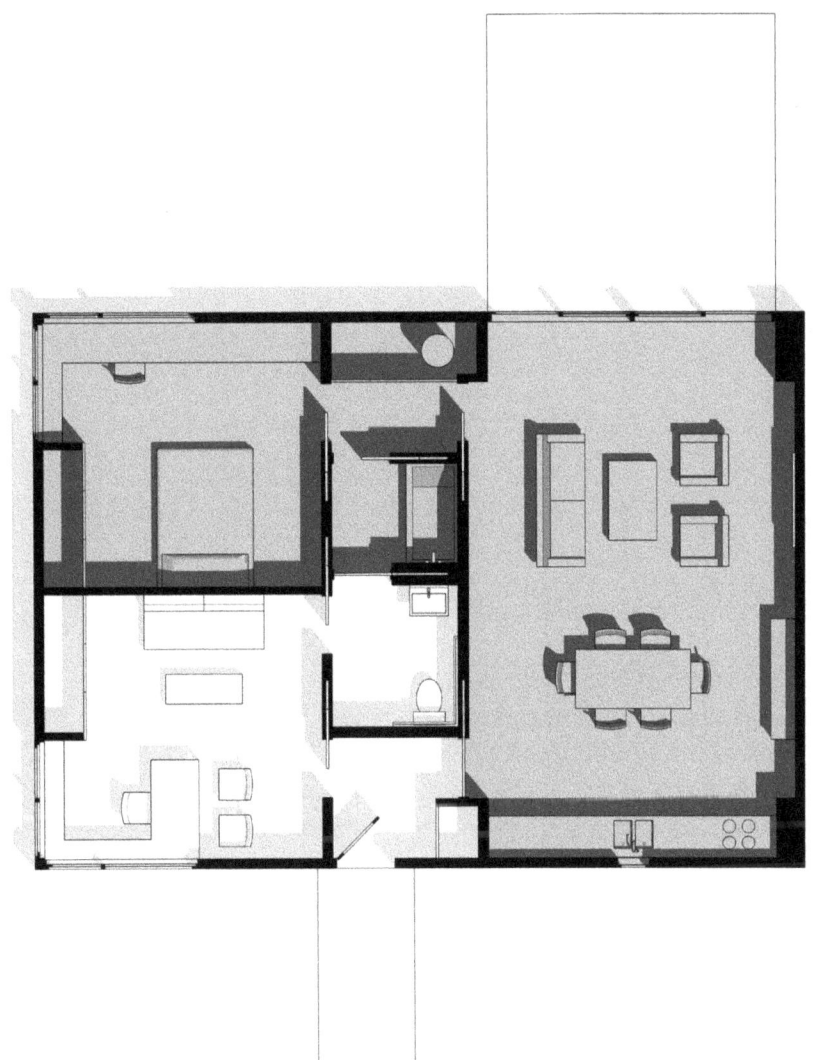

A system of pocket doors opens this plan's entrance, home office, and toilet to visiting clients in isolation from the house's private spaces. The office may also serve as a study/guestroom or second bedroom with direct bathroom access. (Example House A, p. 32.)

17 | Bedroom

Bedroom privacy is less of a concern in a small house occupied by an individual or couple. This presents opportunities to open the sleeping space to the rest of the house and expand its spatial boundary. A bedroom that can have its door left open without overexposing the bed itself may do this quite effectively, especially if the view from living space through the bedroom leads to a window, creating an exterior sightline (opposite, top).

Some iconic modern homes dispense with the bedroom and merely screen the bed from view, effectively adding a room's worth of space to the living area (Ch. 38 and 39).

Bedrooms can add functionality to a small house by accommodating additional uses. Part of a bedroom may be furnished as a workspace or sitting area, providing privacy, quiet, or solitude from the living area.

A second bedroom can serve as a home office, study, or workshop with a daybed for overnight guests (opposite, top). Bedrooms strictly for visitors can sit vacant except for rare occasions — "empty guest chambers for empty guests," as Thoreau mocked them in *Walden*. Designing them for other possible uses ensures a fully vital house.

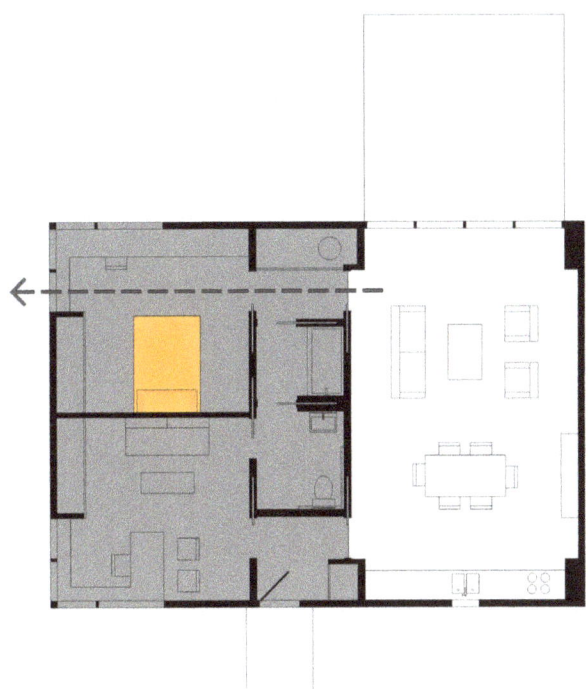

A small house's attitude toward bedrooms is a major design determinant. A bed may fall in a service zone (shaded in plans at left) along with the entryway, bathroom, storage and other secondary spaces (top) or in the more open, served zone of living functions, screened from their view (bottom). If the sleeping space falls in a service zone, it should be designed to allow uncluttered exterior views through it from the living area so that it still contributes to the daytime space of the house. (Example House A, top, p. 32, and Example House C, bottom, p. 88.)

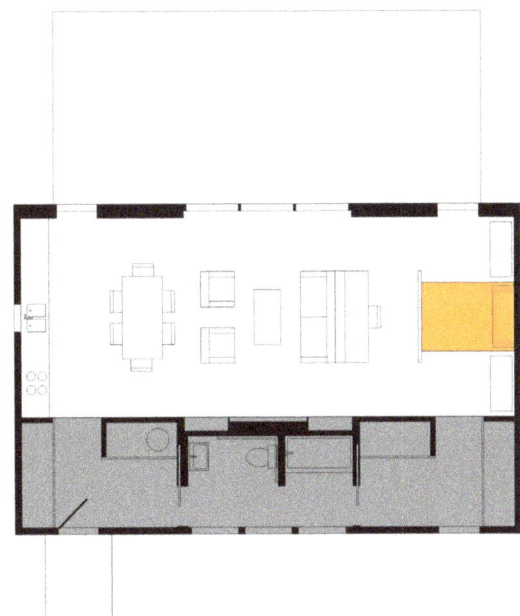

18 | Kitchen

An open combination of kitchen, dining, and living space makes sense as the heart of a compact home. A linear, single-galley kitchen is adequate for a small house and the most spatially efficient solution.

A kitchen island, while a must for many, consumes a significant amount of additional space for maneuvering around it. It also largely duplicates a dining table. Placing an adjustable-height dining table where an island would stand provides the function of both without sacrificing space. A dual-height, combination-island-and-dining table will also save space.

The front wall of a small house can be a dramatic location for a kitchen. With a tall enough ceiling, a high bank of windows over the kitchen can provide private sky views and a flood of natural light balancing that from a more open rear wall (Ch. 44). This ample daylighting serves the kitchen's workspace role and makes it a bright domestic focus.

The side wall of a house may also work well as a kitchen location, allowing it to be near both the house's entrance and an outdoor dining area on a rear terrace. The private rear wall of a small house should typically be reserved for large openings and terrace access.

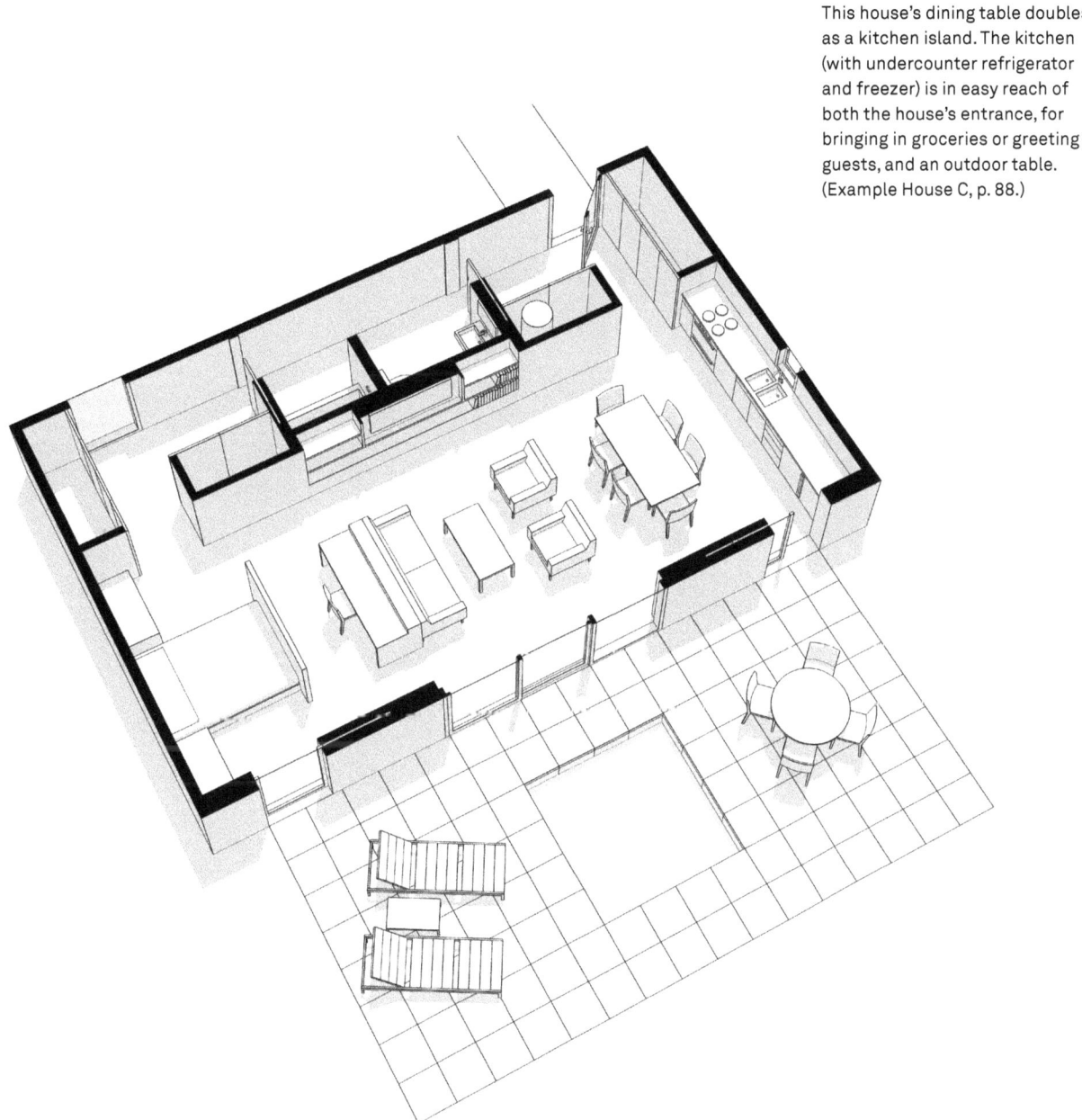

This house's dining table doubles as a kitchen island. The kitchen (with undercounter refrigerator and freezer) is in easy reach of both the house's entrance, for bringing in groceries or greeting guests, and an outdoor table. (Example House C, p. 88.)

19 | Bathroom

A one-bedroom, one-bath, single-story house can efficiently minimize corridors if the bathroom has two doors, one opening onto the sleeping side of the house, the other onto the more public side.

While it's a bit inelegant for a bathroom to open onto an entry space, this arrangement can contribute to a compact plan, especially in a house that absorbs entryway and bathroom in the same service zone.

A window for natural light and ventilation is desirable in a bathroom, but designing for one doesn't always result in the best house plan. If a bathroom is placed away from exterior walls so that open space can loop expansively around it, as in Mies van der Rohe's Farnsworth House (Ch. 38), a window isn't possible.

Locating a bathroom and kitchen back to back for consolidation of plumbing is economical, but less important in a compact house where pipes can't get very far from each other in any case and spatial efficiency is more critical. Modest savings in plumbing will soon be forgotten, but the floor plan is for the life of the house.

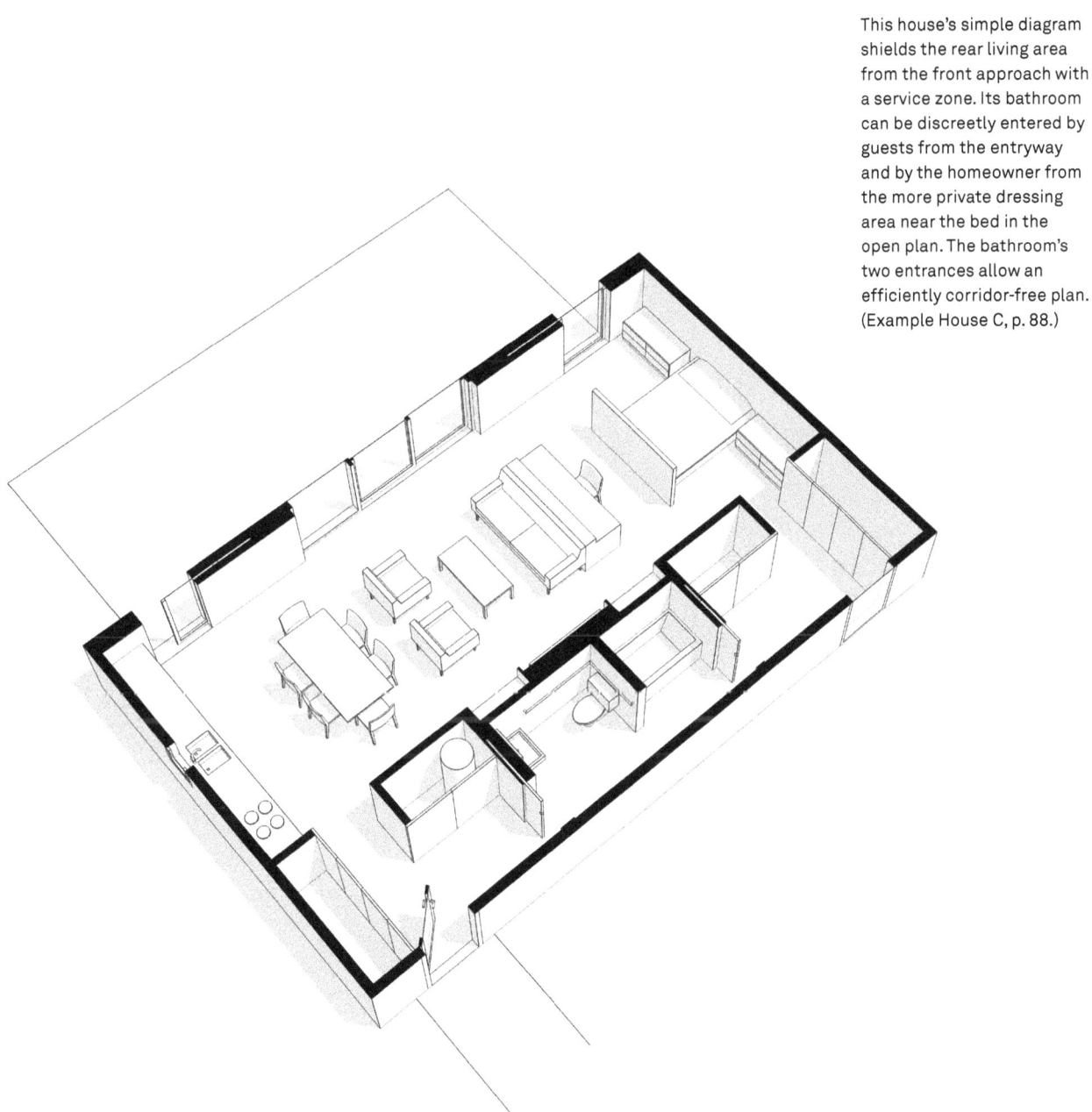

This house's simple diagram shields the rear living area from the front approach with a service zone. Its bathroom can be discreetly entered by guests from the entryway and by the homeowner from the more private dressing area near the bed in the open plan. The bathroom's two entrances allow an efficiently corridor-free plan. (Example House C, p. 88.)

20 | Storage

George Carlin wasn't entirely joking when he said "a house is just a place to keep your stuff while you go out and get more stuff." Storage capacity is essential for any house, but especially a small one more vulnerable to crowding by ever-accumulating possessions.

Storage items include those we want to hide and those we want to enshrine. Utilitarian storage is best provided by closets two feet deep or slightly more. These should be organized within service zones laid out in a house's generative design diagram. They can line corridors or occupy thickened exterior walls inappropriate for windows, like those facing next-door neighbors. Such closets are more efficient than walk-in storage rooms with their inside maneuvering space stolen from a small house's potential open area. Storage walls are also opportunities for alcoves to contain furniture pieces or worktops, or absorb a single-galley kitchen.

Storage of books, collections, or prized possessions should be located to complement furniture arrangements and avoid damage from weather and direct sunlight. Planning their accommodation and display creates order and calm where clutter and visual noise might prevail. Like well-designed furniture (Ch. 26), high-quality storage products such as the flexible and sustainably reusable 606 Universal Shelving System designed by Dieter Rams can make an architectural statement as effectively as costly built-ins, justifying their purchase cost.

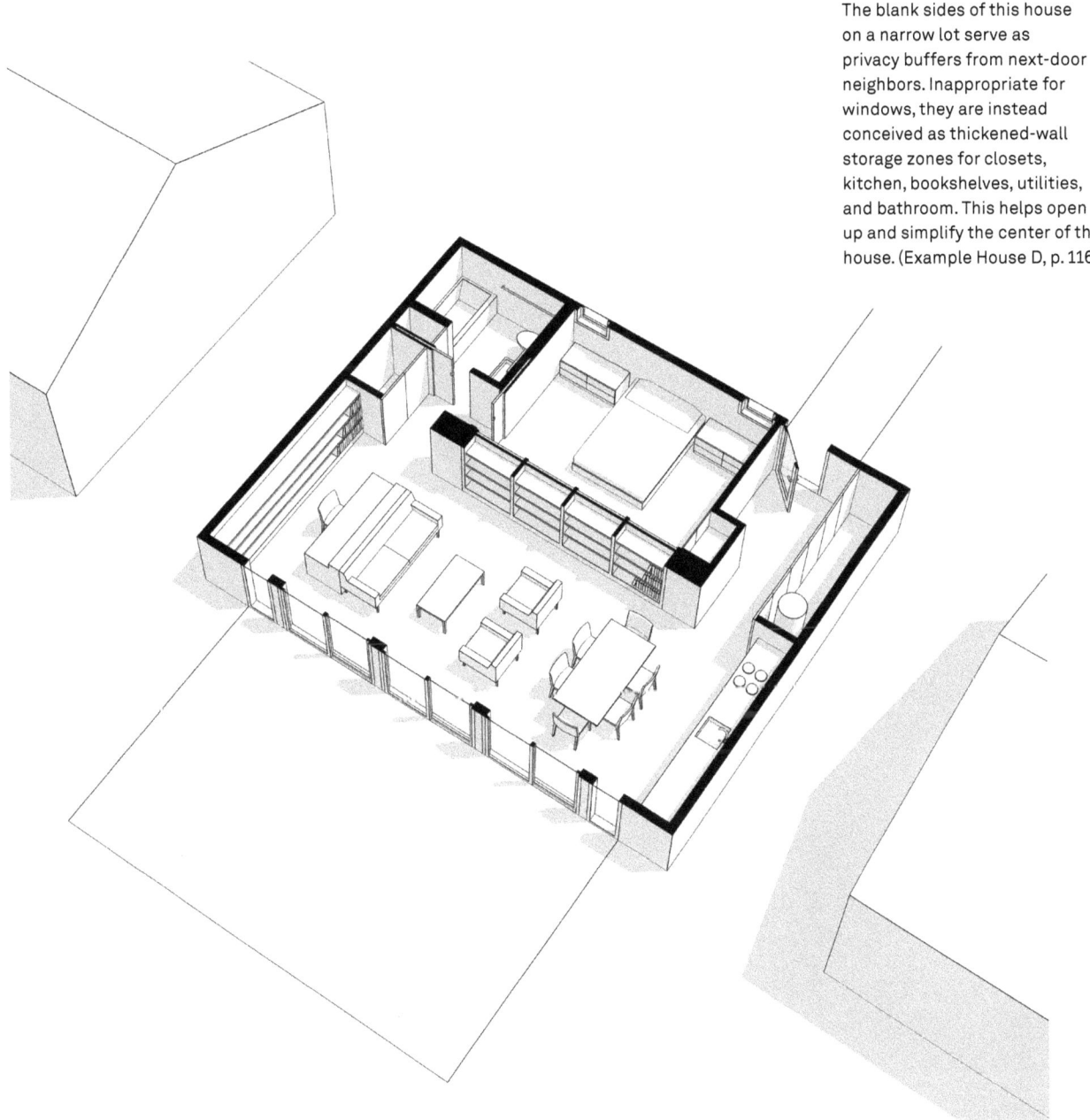

The blank sides of this house on a narrow lot serve as privacy buffers from next-door neighbors. Inappropriate for windows, they are instead conceived as thickened-wall storage zones for closets, kitchen, bookshelves, utilities, and bathroom. This helps open up and simplify the center of the house. (Example House D, p. 116.)

Example

B

38' x 26'
988 square feet
10' & 7' ceilings

Like the Farnsworth House (Ch. 38) and Philip Johnson's Glass House (Ch. 39), this design maintains the spirit of a one-room pavilion by containing services—here the kitchen, bath, and bed—in an island-like core around which the entire space of the house freely flows. Unlike its fully glass-walled antecedents, this house's exterior walls are thickened to house storage, a workspace, and a dining banquette created by daybeds with removable bolsters for overnight guests. The house's perimeter is broken open by glass where it matters most, the four corners that would otherwise define a constraining box (Ch. 36 and 37). As in the Farnsworth House, the walls of the central service core stop short of the ceiling to make it more like a freestanding piece of furniture than partitioning architecture. A cylindrical "chimney" rising above this core carries kitchen and bathroom exhaust through the roof. Aside from closets, the only interior door is that of the bathroom. The living area has long views past the core, which screens the bed. Not sealed in its own room, the sleeping area becomes part of the house's greater space. This makes the nearby workspace feel more like a place in the house than in a bedroom, similar to the desk near the bed in Philip Johnson's Glass House (Ch. 39).

Example B
Plan

Example B
Low plan perspective from front/side

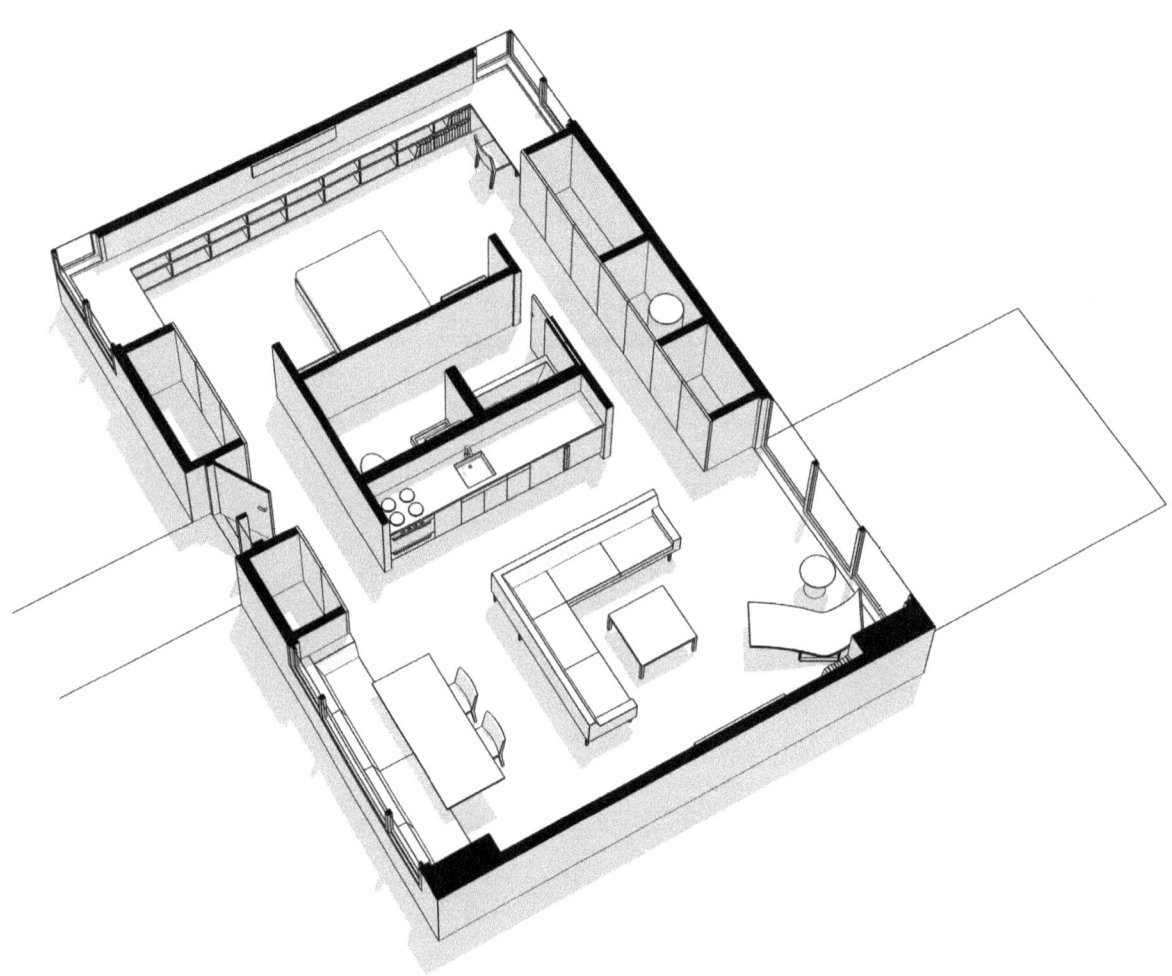

Example B
High plan perspective from rear/side

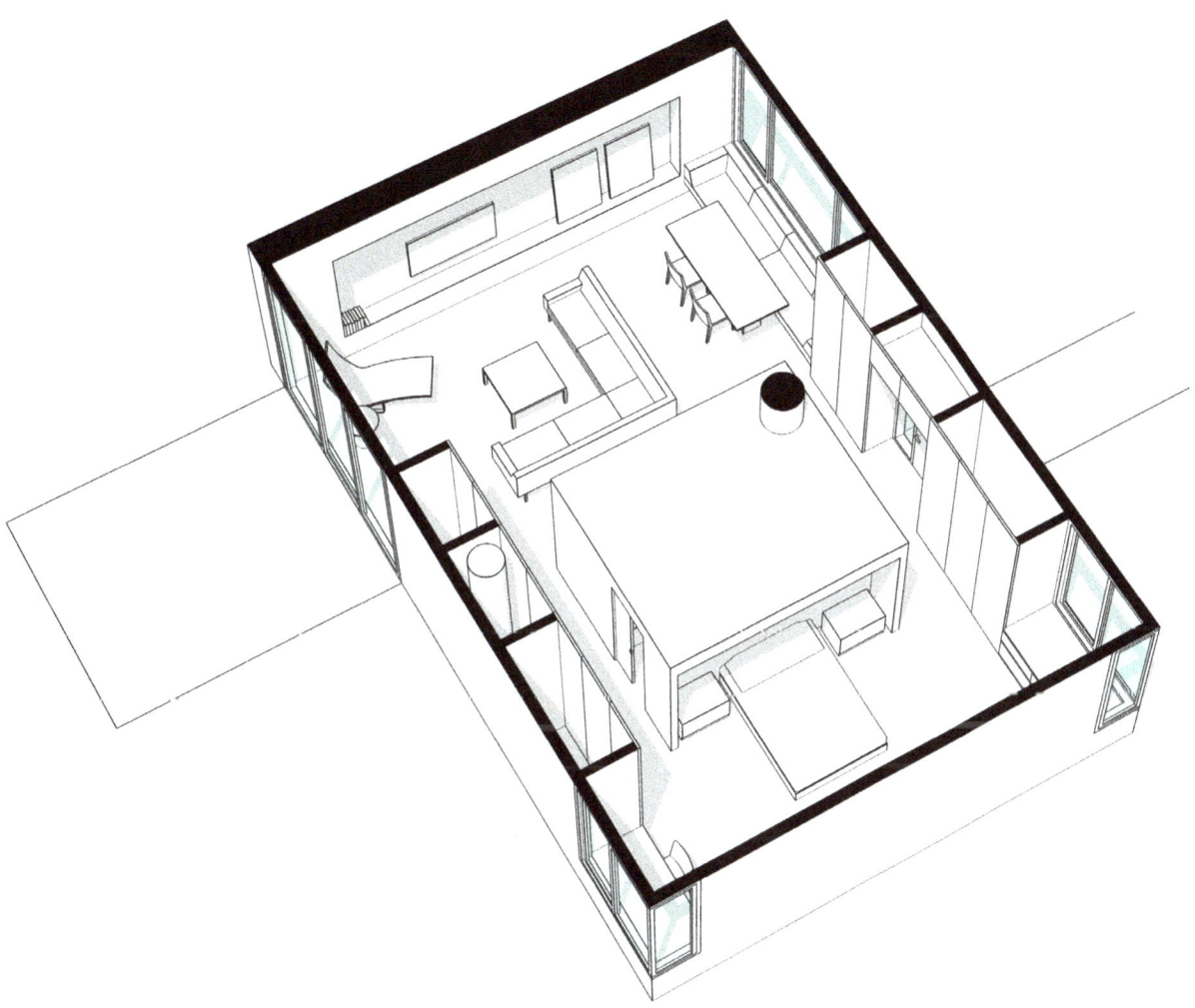

Example B
Front

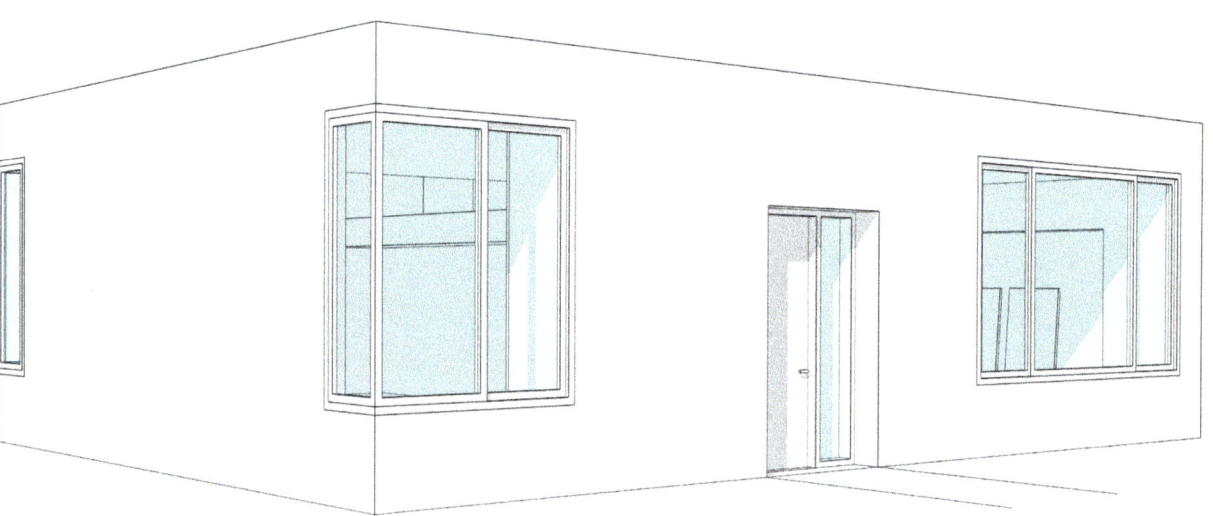

Example B
Rear

Example B
Top: Section key plan
Bottom: Section B-B

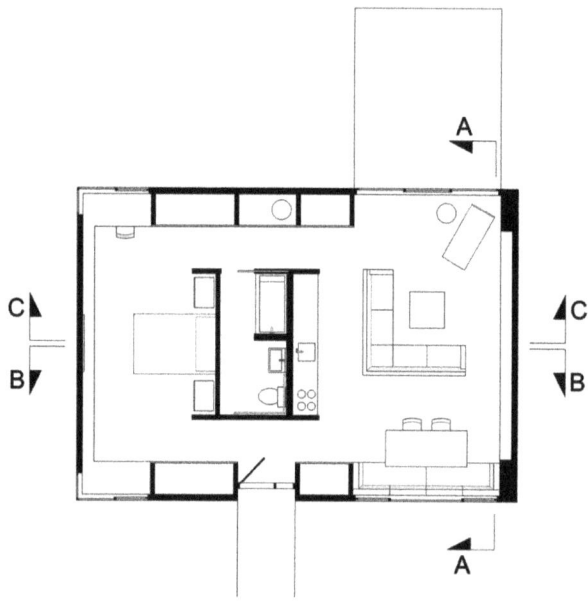

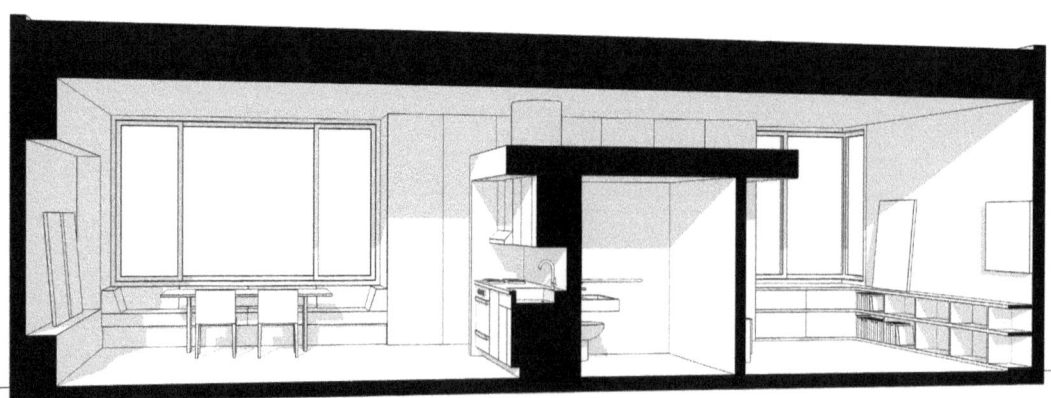

Example B
Top: Section A-A
Bottom: Section C-C

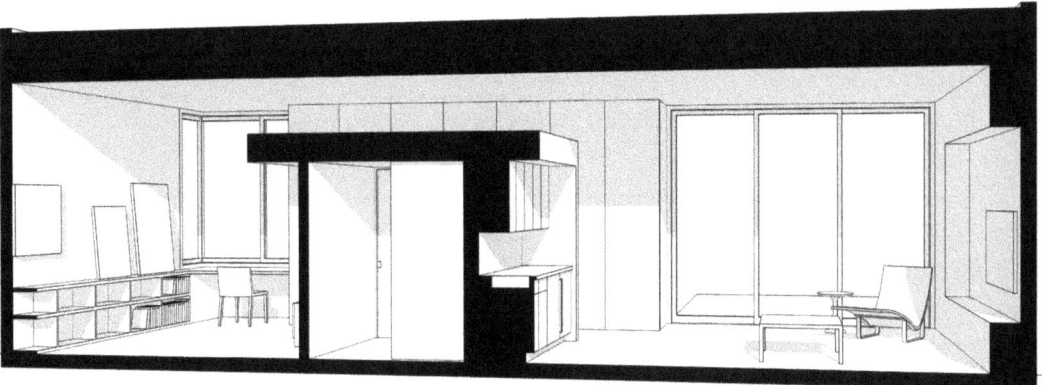

21 | Door

Doors accentuate a house's compartmentalization into what Frank Lloyd Wright called a box full of room-boxes. Minimizing their contribution to this effect will make a small house feel less confining.

Ceiling-height doors can be abstracted to read more as floor-to-ceiling wall panels and less like ship hatches when closed. When open, such doors enhance the continuity of rooms, allowing both floor and ceiling planes — and sense of space — to flow from one to the next. Placed at wall intersections, they can break the box of a room by fully removing its defining corners (Ch. 24).

Openings in bearing walls require lintels spanning their tops, which prevent floor-to-ceiling doors. This limitation can be overcome by raising lintels above ceiling level into the depth of roof construction. As an alternative, long-span roof rafters or trusses can eliminate the need for interior bearing walls altogether. Such solutions are less feasible with an additional story above — more reason to build a one-story house (Ch. 8).

Sliding pocket doors have the advantage of disappearing when open, while open swinging doors take up space and may block other doors or contribute to a sense of containment just by their visible potential to swing shut. Swinging doors also require more adjacent floor area for wheelchair maneuvering than pocket doors in certain cases. Storage space doors should simulate wall panels by use of concealed or minimally visible hardware to allow visual calm befitting a refuge.

Reducing the number of rooms and doors increases a house's spaciousness. Except for closet doors treated as paneling, this house has only one interior door, for the bathroom. The bed is screened from view rather than given its own room, making the interior a single expansive space. (Example House B, p. 60.)

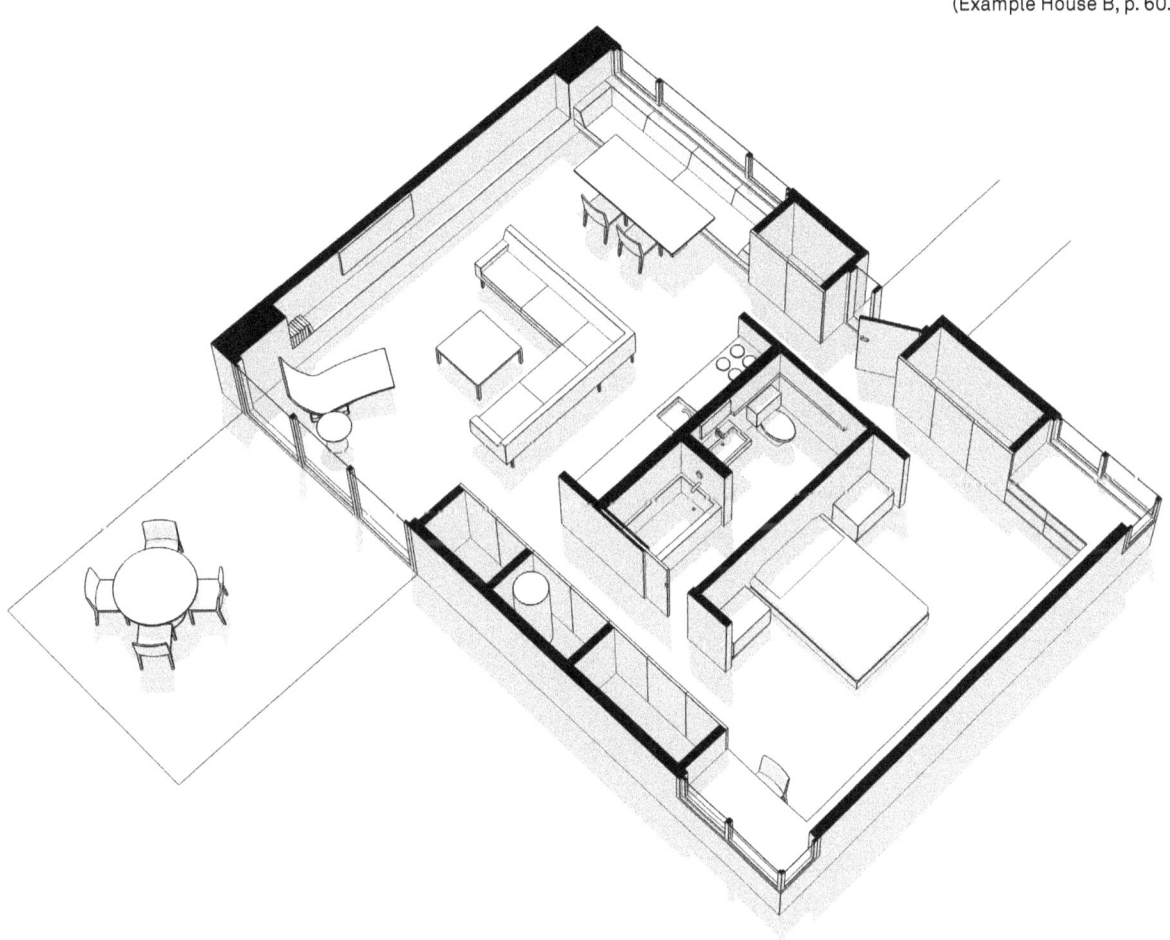

22 | Window

One advantage of a small house is that daylight doesn't need to penetrate far to reach its center. Natural light stimulates serotonin, the mood-regulating neurotransmitter which increases alertness, learning ability, and feelings of well-being.

    Windows on multiple sides of a space allow cross ventilation and approximate the ambient light of the sky canopy under which we evolved — the light in which we still perform best. Opposite-side daylight sources also counter glare. Even a small window across from a wall of glass will soften harsh shadows like a photographer's fill light. The same small window will provide outsize spatial release by conveying the presence of the great outdoors just beyond the wall it pierces. Providing windows on only one side of a space creates a cave-like interior and denies us awareness of encircling outdoor space.

    Tall ceilings allow for high windows that let light fall deeper inside and let us see more sky. Elevated windows can be placed where lower ones might compromise privacy, providing controlled views above neighboring buildings or traffic. Windows should be deployed at focal points like the ends of long, eye-leading, interior prospects to continue a small house's space outdoors. Where privacy is a concern, translucent glass can still provide daylight and expansively convey space beyond.

    Windows placed at corners not only break the box and enhance the outdoor flow of interior space (Ch. 37), but allow light to flood in over adjacent walls, providing the illuminated backdrop and transfiguring presence found in a Vermeer painting (Ch. 27).

Edward Hopper's 1951 painting, *Rooms by the Sea*, or "The Jumping Off Place" as he tellingly called it in his notebook, demonstrates both how freely light washes in through a corner opening and space propels itself outward. The forlornly circumscribed square of light from a conventional window in the next room speaks of a more typical indoor estrangement from nature.

23 | Window Wall

Without resorting to costly sliding or folding glass walls that seem to disappear, a small house can effectively become its own porch by means of a wall of mulled-together windows and glazed doors. Such assemblies are limited in size and arrangement by code-defined local wind loads. Meeting these may require mullions to have internal steel reinforcement.

    However the effect of a glazed wall is achieved, it can allow a home's indoor living area to expand out onto a terrace, greatly increasing its perceived space and relation to nature. The greatest challenge of such an opening is in spanning across its top. For longer spans than standard wood or light-gauge steel framing can handle, prefabricated portal frames offer the strength of structural steel at a contained expense.

    Many people prefer a south-facing window wall and sun-drenched interior, but facing north reduces glare and the damaging effects of direct sunlight, while looking out on an appealingly front-lit prospect—the preferred orientation of the artist's studio.

    The expense of a window wall filling one side of a high-ceilinged living space is easily justified by its return in space, light, grandeur, and quality of daily life. It's worth building a smaller house just to afford these rewards.

Posts subdivide this large opening into manageable spans economically filled by conventional sliding glass doors with transoms. (Example House D, p. 116.)

24 | Space Traps

Inside corners carry a sense of constraint which it's critical to minimize in a small house. They trap space and stop the eye's sweep at places of decidedly unmystical emptiness. We have an inbred dislike of corners; our primitive ancestors would have avoided them as places of potential entrapment. Misbehaving children are made to stand in them.

Corners can be broken open with passages, or door or window openings. Their dead space can also be filled with built-in shelving or seating, or other signs of life which add depth and utility.

Corridors may have the same backwater lifelessness as corners, especially if they lead the eye to a dead end. A very compact house can eliminate corridors altogether. Where they are necessary, windows at or near their ends can admit natural light and suggest exterior escape. If a living area's view down a passageway ends at the door to a room, the design should allow for the door to remain open as much as possible without exposing private contents or clutter. The line of sight through the passage, the open door, and the room should then ideally continue outside through a window, creating an exterior sightline.

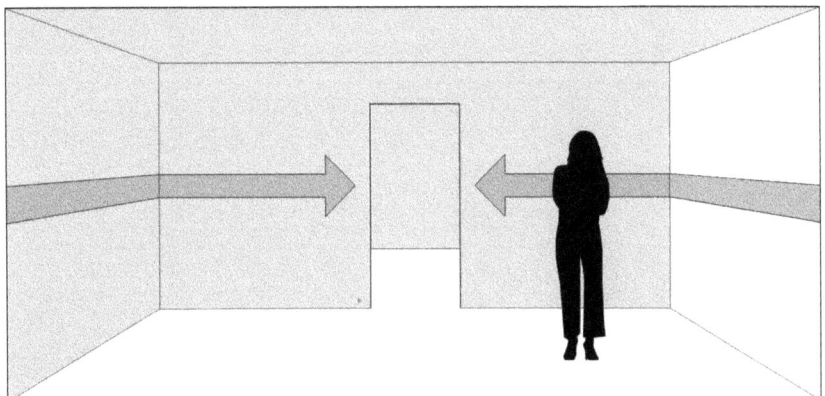

Space flows in the direction of its containing walls, as corridors prove. Corners interrupt flow. The visual release into space beyond provided by a punched opening is at right angles to the momentum of spatial flow over the surfaces framing the opening.

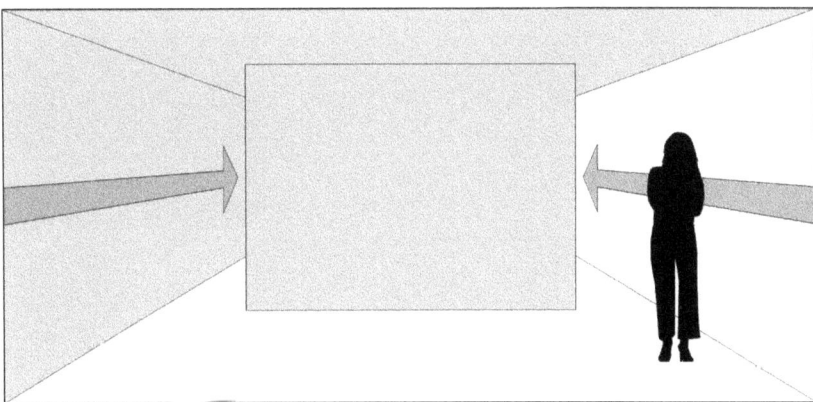

Where floor-to-ceiling openings fully displace corners, space flows unrestricted over walls into further areas, adding its momentum to the sense of release. Space that disappears "around the bend" might be limitlessness.

Space is trapped in corners between walls and floors or ceilings as well. Giving a wall a function turns it from a flat rebuff to an approachable resource.

25 | Alcove

Alcoves allow an interior space to contain subsidiary functions without losing a simple, unified overall shape. This applies if, in the manner of classical apses or niches, they don't rise to the full height of the room they occupy but let its upper reaches and ceiling define its basic shape.

If an exterior wall of a house is thickened (Ch. 42) to form a service zone a few feet deep, it can absorb a bank of closets interrupted by an alcove for a desk, console, open shelving, daybed for overnight guests or other amenity. Such alcoves also provide opportunities for smaller windows.

Alcoves can either fully contain an element like a single-galley kitchen (Ch. 18) or part of a furniture grouping, like a banquette or bench seat for a dining table. Using alcoves to eliminate or reduce projections into the volume of a living space can make it feel less cramped and allow more generous pathways through it, amplifying a small house without diminishing its simple appeal.

At night, a lamp-lit alcove can create a hearth-like pocket of illumination and visual warmth (Ch. 28).

Alcoves can accommodate furniture or built-ins, or provide space to pass around central furniture groupings. They expand the inhabited lower stratum of a tall space without adding to the width and cost of a wall-to-wall window assembly which conveys full-bore exterior openness and admits a Vermeer-like wash of daylight (Ch. 22 and 27). (Example House A, p. 32.)

26 | Furniture

Before a house is designed, the optimal building-site location for its living space's chairs, tables and desks should be determined, based on views, privacy, natural light, and the opportunity for an adjacent terrace. The design process should begin with this furniture because the finished house will be judged from its vantage. This is a much simpler and more defining act for a small house with one living area.

Low furniture conveys repose and amplifies ceiling height, adding to the perceived volume of a small house. Clean lines create visual quiet and calm in keeping with the ideal of home as refuge. Pieces on high legs and open below emphasize the continuity of the floor plane and allow its full expanse to define the limits of a space. A similar effect is achieved by placing furniture away from walls to let the uninterrupted sweep of their planes convey the full spatial envelope.

Furniture plays roles beyond its immediate function. Notably well-designed pieces can stand almost as artworks and substitute for costly construction details in setting a house's tone; the simpler the house, the greater their impact in determining its character. Furniture groupings are tableaus which populate space with human presence and behavior even when vacant. They lend composition and attitude to the blank canvas of a space. Needing less furniture, small houses invite spending more on fewer but better pieces. Furniture is integral to a house's architecture and should be included in its construction budget.

Philip Johnson's Glass House is built around pieces by Mies van der Rohe and Lilly Reich, who had decorated his Manhattan apartment. He adapted their furniture selection and arrangement for the apartment's living room as the kernel of his new house, designing outward from it in what he called a series of nested boxes: "It starts with the coffee table. That is the first unit, and that has never changed. A carefully designed living room that is outlined by the edge of the white rug. The white rug is a raft. The living room is the next box, and the living room sits in a bigger living room." (Ch. 39).

27 | White

In his 1954 book, *The Natural House*, Frank Lloyd Wright advised against paint altogether, preferring a palette of native material colors: "Wood is wood, concrete is concrete, stone is stone." When it comes to affordable sheetrock, though, a paint color must be chosen.

    Color has spatial implications that are especially important in a small-house interior. It's an often challenged truism that white makes a space feel larger. Dissenters argue that dark surfaces visually recede and the tyranny of the white-minded substitutes sterility for personal expression. There are other arguments for white. Colors are defined by the wavelengths of the visible spectrum they absorb rather than reflect. In reflecting all, white bounces more light around a space than any color. It maximizes ambient natural light. This boosts serotonin levels in the brain, improving mood and performance, while suggesting outdoor rather than indoor experience. Sunlight is the fundamental element of the natural world that made and first housed us; it makes us feel at home on the deepest level.

    White's neutrality intensifies the color of people and objects as well as outdoor nature, our ever-changing native decor. It clashes with nothing. No color so sensitively registers changing atmospheric conditions — whether passing clouds, oncoming storms, golden sunsets, or the wind we see in stirred tree shadows — keeping us in the moment and mindful of our place in the cosmos.

    White has a liberating, universal quality. Psychologically, it's a blank page on which to start a new chapter every day.

In Johannes Vermeer's *Woman with a Pearl Necklace* (1664), the mystery of light's immaterial, colorless essence renders an everyday domestic scene sublime.

28 | Night

The character of a house changes dramatically at night when windows darken and leave us bounded in the nutshell of its interior. Early humans returned from a day of hunting and gathering to the nighttime campfire and its circle of light, an intimate setting that a small house is well suited to recapture.

Fireplaces appeal to our inherited sensibilities but aren't environmentally friendly, while much of their effect can be achieved with low, warmly shaded lighting that attenuates into shadow like the campfire's glow. Ceiling light fixtures can seem to press down on and over-illuminate an interior, emphasizing its containing surfaces in the absence of relieving outdoor views, while denying us the experience of night and disrupting our diurnal rhythm. Bright artificial light suppresses evening production of melatonin, the hormone that regulates the sleep-wake cycle. This effect can persist even after lights are turned out.

Artificial light should focus attention on cherished possessions and recast interiors in a transforming range of highlights and shadows. A lamp can serve as a focal point itself, echoing the campfire.

The lighting in Sir Edward John Poynter's *An Evening at Home* (1888) creates a mood of intimacy and end-of-day relaxation.

29 | *Walden*

Henry David Thoreau's account of cabin life at Walden Pond is the small-house bible:

> If one designs to construct a dwelling house, it behooves him to exercise a little Yankee shrewdness, lest after all he find himself in a workhouse, a labyrinth without a clew, a museum, an almshouse, a prison, or a splendid mausoleum instead. Consider first how slight a shelter is absolutely necessary.
>
> And when the farmer has got his house, he may not be the richer but the poorer for it, and it be the house that has got him.
>
> Our houses are such unwieldy property that we are often imprisoned rather than housed in them.
>
> Most men appear never to have considered what a house is, and are actually though needlessly poor all their lives because they think they must have such a one as their neighbors have.
>
> I went into the woods because I wished to live deliberately, to front only on the essential facts of life, and see if I could not learn what it had to teach, and not, when I came to die, discover that I had not lived.... I wanted to live deep and suck out all the marrow of life, to live so sturdily and Spartan-like as to put to rout all that was not life.
>
> Our life is frittered away by detail.... Simplify, simplify.

WALDEN;

OR,

LIFE IN THE WOODS.

By HENRY D. THOREAU,
AUTHOR OF "A WEEK ON THE CONCORD AND MERRIMACK RIVERS."

I do not propose to write an ode to dejection, but to brag as lustily as chanticleer in the morning, standing on his roost, if only to wake my neighbors up. — Page 92.

BOSTON:
TICKNOR AND FIELDS.
M DCCC LIV.

Walden (1854) is one of America's most celebrated literary works. Its enduring appeal speaks of an abiding popular crosscurrent against materialism.

30 | Contentment

Of material luxuries, Thoreau asks in *Walden*, "Shall we always study to obtain more of these things, and not sometimes be content with less?"

Studies show that when something desired is obtained, the expected happiness rarely ensues. This is nature's plan: finding happiness would stop us in our tracks, while constant discontent and the pursuit of happiness keep us moving on to fresher pastures. It's why the grass is always greener on the other side. While this kept our ancestors fed, it only keeps us hungry.

Many of our inherited priorities concern reproduction. Male bowerbirds display their fitness as mates and attract females by building structures of sticks and brightly colored objects — the animal kingdom's dueling McMansions. We're programmed to constantly measure our material possessions against those of others, especially competitors within view — the Joneses down the street who must be kept up with — because they're within our inner bowerbird's mating radius. Falling behind activates a vestigial fear of extinction. Now that courtship only works like this for flashy narcissists and their serial trophy mates, the rest of us are free to drop out and smell the roses.

The protagonist of F. Scott Fitzgerald's *The Great Gatsby* pursues the woman of his dreams by scrapping his way up the social ladder and building a mansion in sight of the one she shares with her rich husband. Like happiness's false promise, she betrays him, proving superficial and unworthy of his effort.

I thought of Gatsby's wonder when he first picked out the green light at the end of Daisy's dock. He had come a long way to this blue lawn, and his dream must have seemed so close that he could hardly fail to grasp it.... Gatsby believed in the green light, the orgastic future that year by year recedes before us. It eluded us then, but that's no matter — tomorrow we will run faster, stretch out our arms farther.... And one fine morning —

So we beat on, boats against the current, borne back ceaselessly into the past.

F. Scott Fitzgerald, *The Great Gatsby*

We evolved in an environment where status was highly correlated with reproductive success, and material resources were always scarce. Thus our motivational psychology tells us to compete for status and to acquire resources. We might think we want to do it because it will make us happy. Actually, we want to do it because our most successful ancestors were the ones who wanted to, and the bit about happiness is a kind of mirage.

Daniel Nettle, *Happiness: The Science Behind Your Smile*

Life is a progress from want to want, not from enjoyment to enjoyment.

Boswell's *Life of Johnson*

Example

C

38' x 24'
912 square feet
12' & 8' ceilings

The front of this house is conceived as a thickened wall containting an entry hall, bathroom, dressing area, and storage while forming a barrier between the street and private rear living spaces. The front door has translucent glazing for privacy and a high clear-glass transom above, where privacy is less of a concern. These allow natural light to wash past the front service zone into the living area, balancing the illumination from rear windows. They also provide spatial release at what would be a constraining corner. This is answered at the other end of the front of the house by a symmetrically placed translucent front window with a matching clear transom. These full-height front openings add an expansive sense of outdoor space flowing through the house front-to-back. The front service zone is a concealed backstage for the luxuriously long, serene, one-room living-sleeping area. The kitchen and bed occupy alcoves, reducing their spatial intrusion and aiding the effect of wall-to-wall glass in back (Section C-C, p. 95). Together with the allocation of rear windows to corners and a central seating area, this effect creates much of the impact of a fully open rear wall onto a terrace, where half this wall is actually solid.

Example C

Plan

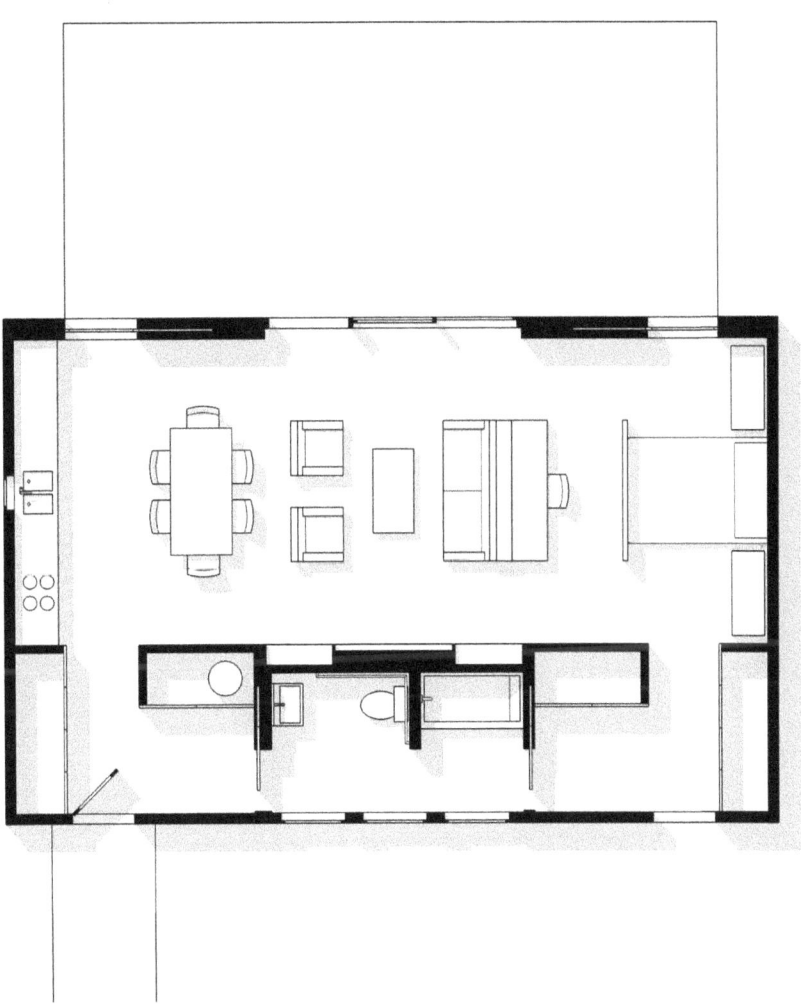

Example C
Low plan perspective from front

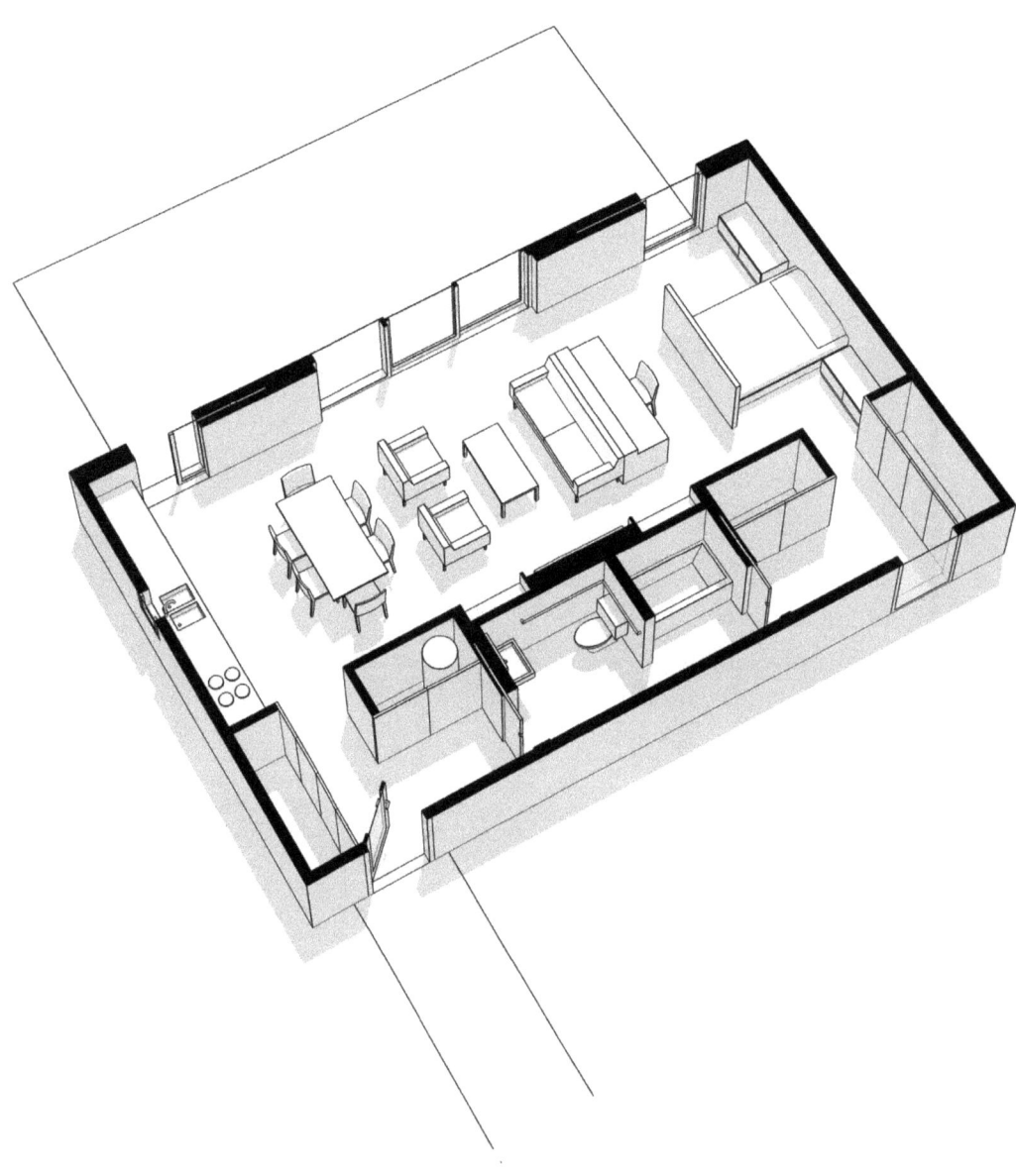

Example C
High plan perspective from rear

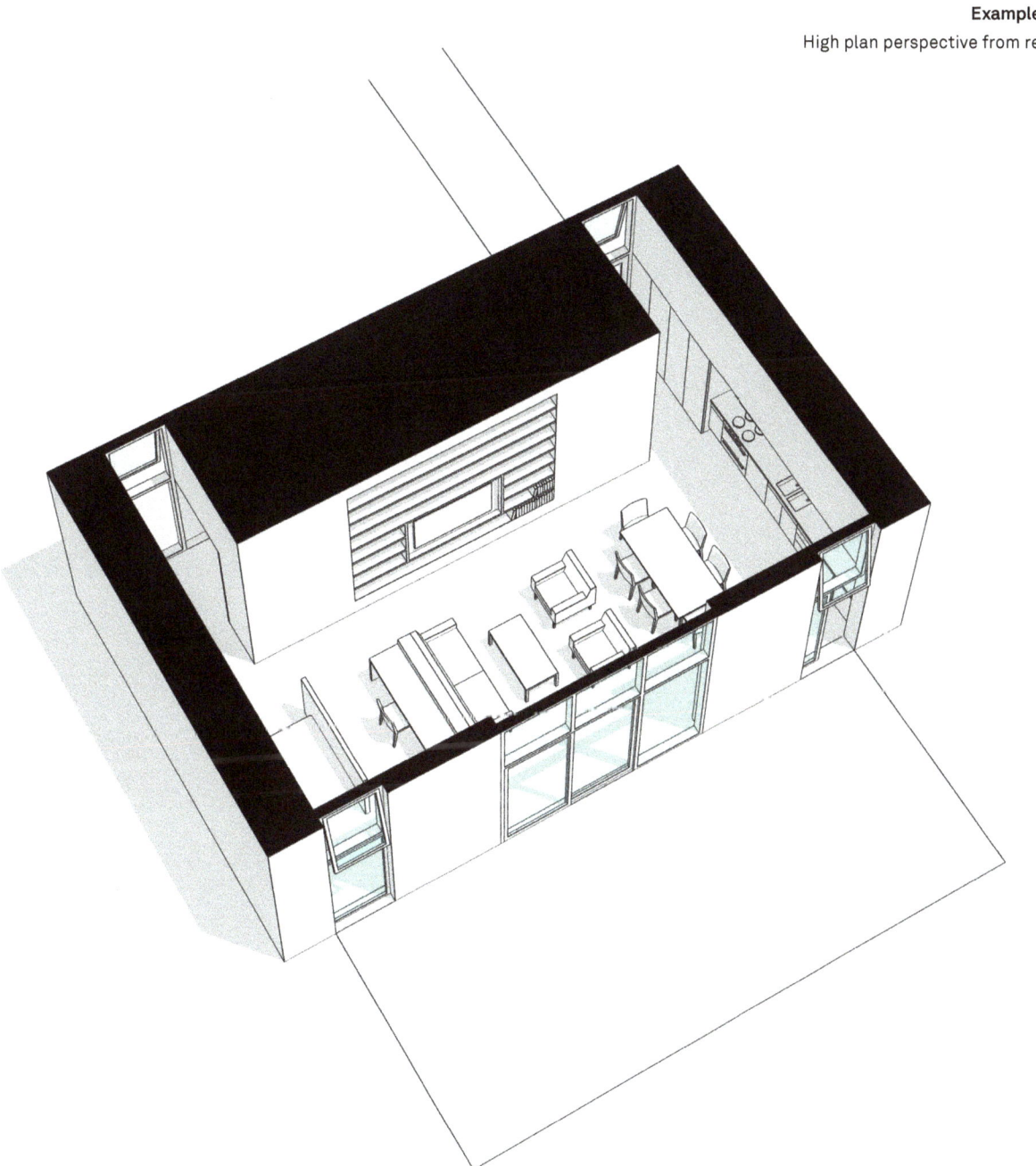

Example C
Front

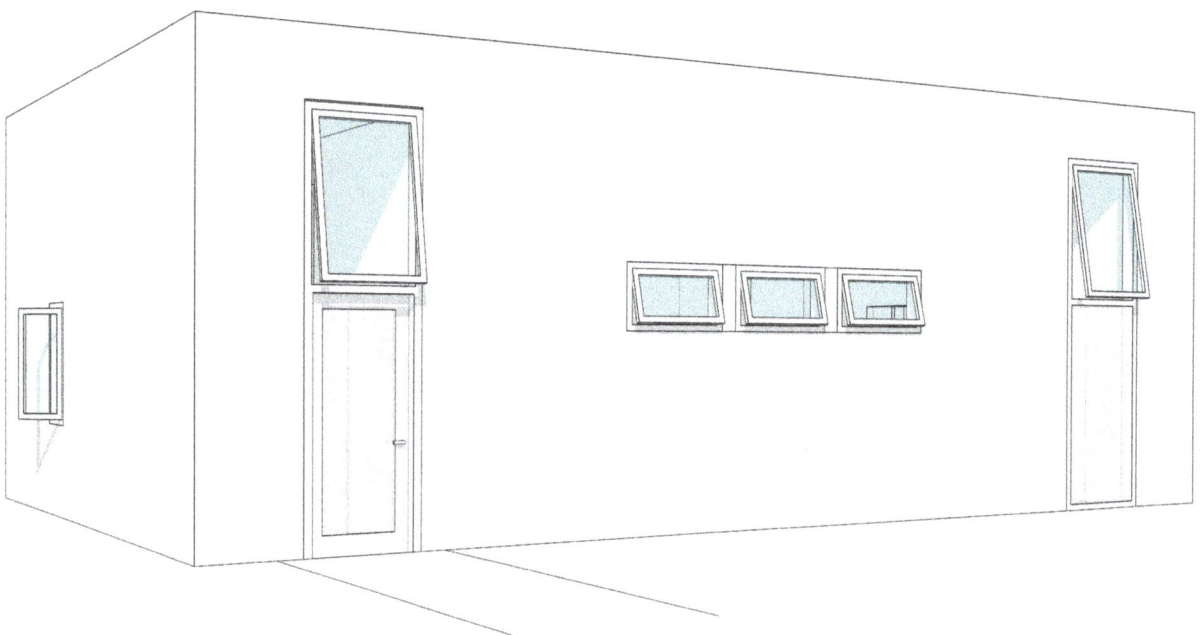

Example C
Rear

Example C
Top: Section key plan
Bottom: Section B-B

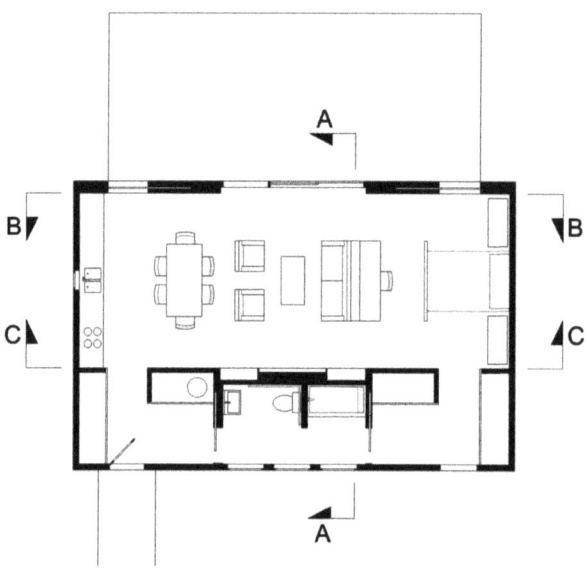

Example C
Top: Section A-A
Bottom: Section C-C

31 | Evolution

Evolutionary psychology is an invaluable tool for the design of a home. To understand that historic scarcity, not current need, underlies our materialism is to know it will never be satisfied. This realization frees us from our bottomless craving for more. It lets us be content with a small house that indulges our love of nature by minimizing what separates us from it.

Accommodating our instinct for outdoor exposure has demonstrable merit and should inform the design process. The restorative power of nature long claimed by poets, philosophers, and park advocates has now been proven in studies linking student test scores to classroom daylight levels and views of greenery. Features of our ancestral habitat still catalyze brain chemistry, affecting our experience of life more directly than any material possession or architectural style.

Other sensitivities traceable to the forest, grassland, and campfire may be irrational today but carry undeniable subconscious weight which it would be foolish to ignore. Designing around them can make us feel at home on the deepest level and restore our vitality.

We may imagine a time when, in the infancy of the human race, some enterprising mortal crept into a hollow in a rock for shelter. Every child begins the world again, to some extent, and loves to stay out doors, even in wet and cold. It plays house … having an instinct for it. Who does not remember the interest with which when young he looked at shelving rocks, or any approach to a cave? It was the natural yearning of that portion of our most primitive ancestor which still survived in us. From the cave we have advanced to roofs of palm leaves, of barks and boughs, of linen woven and stretched, of grass and straw, of boards and shingles, of stones and tiles. At last, we know not what it is to live in open air, and our lives are domestic in more senses than we think. From the hearth to the field is a great distance. It would be well perhaps if we were to spend more of our days and nights without any obstruction between us and the celestial bodies, if the poet did not speak so much from under a roof, or the saint dwell so long there. Birds do not sing in caves, nor do doves cherish their innocence in dovecots.

Henry David Thoreau, *Walden*

32 | Prospect-Refuge

In his 1975 book, *The Experience of Landscape*, geographer Jay Appleton defined *prospect* as the ability to see without being seen and *refuge* as the ability to hide. Primitive man, sometimes stealthy hunter and sometimes stalked prey, had a mortal stake in these capacities. Our inherited sensitivity to prospect and refuge persists in the dollar value of a home's views and seclusion, and our uneasiness with unseen basements, crawlspaces, attics, and even spare rooms.

Architectural historian Grant Hildebrand applied Appleton's concept, now called prospect-refuge theory, to Frank Lloyd Wright's houses in his 1991 book, *The Wright Space*. Hildebrand saw refuge in the indirect entrances and cave-like hearths of Wright's houses, and prospect in their heavily glazed perimeters, and terraces (Ch. 14 and 15).

Mies van der Rohe's glass-walled Farnsworth House (Ch. 13) shifted the ideal of residential luxury from the opacity of refuge to the clarity of prospect. On a visit to the Glass House designed by Mies's disciple Philip Johnson (Ch. 47), Frank Lloyd Wright mocked, "I don't know whether I'm supposed to take off my hat or leave it on. Am I indoors or outdoors?" While this was just what Johnson intended, Wright considered privacy an essential part of shelter and saw in the Glass House only prospect, not refuge. For Johnson, the trees surrounding his house formed its screening walls and spatial extent; he called its park-like setting "very expensive wallpaper." In this privileged conception, prospect and refuge merge.

A domesticated cat with residual hunter instincts enjoys prospect and refuge in Hiroshige's woodblock print, *Asakusa Ricefields and Torinomachi Festival*, No. 101 from *One Hundred Famous Views of Edo* (1857).

33 | Primitive Hut

Architects have long been fascinated by the concept of the Primitive Hut. Children show a similar interest when they improvise play houses. Small-house design should tap the universal appeal of simple shelter.

Marc-Antoine Laugier's 1753 *Essay on Architecture* responded to the excesses of its Baroque era by calling for a more vital and functional architecture to replace artificial systems of ornament and "parts added by caprice." Laugier called for a return to "the simplicity of the first model," the Primitive Hut, built intuitively and unselfconsciously by a still-natural man just emerged from cave and forest who "wants to make himself a dwelling that protects but does not bury him."

The essay's frontispiece shows a female personification of architecture pointing infant mankind the way to a hut so rustic it's partly made of living trees. Like Thoreau's cabin (Ch. 4), it offers an alternative to runaway architecture that partitions us from nature and an authentic life. When Thoreau wrote in *Walden* that increasingly substantial homes have made our lives "domestic in more senses than we think," he played on the word's old meaning of "domesticated." Like house cats, we've had much of our true nature tamed out of us by indoor existence. As the undomesticated — and uncorrupted — Huck Finn says of life with his guardian the Widow Douglas who would "sivilize" him, "it was rough living in the house all the time."

Laugier's open-sided hut is also a pavilion, a one-room archetype and touchstone for architecturally significant modern houses.

The frontispiece of Laugier's canonic *Essay on Architecture* is one of architectural theory's most famous images.

34 | Pavilion

Removing partitions expands the interior space of a house, making it more like a pavilion — an open-sided, one-space structure with a roof held up by posts, like a garden tent or Laugier's image of the Primitive Hut (Ch. 33).

This simple building type contrasts with the conventional house Frank Lloyd Wright denounced as a complicated box of smaller room-boxes. His own houses typically feature a pavilion-like main space combining living functions under a unifying and sometimes even tent-like ceiling (Ch. 14).

Mies van der Rohe's Farnsworth House (Ch. 38) and Philip Johnson's Glass House (Ch. 39) are more authentic pavilions. Their plans dispense with partitions altogether to create an interior the full size of the house. Individual rooms with pigeonholing functional assignments give way to the blank slate Mies called "universal space." This honors the classic concept of the pavilion as a single room without a specific role, built instead for pleasure.

Just as we may feel diminished when identified by our occupations, a house's spaces are debased by their limiting designation as "dining room" or "bedroom." Whether or not they abolish rooms and their officious job titles altogether, pavilion-inspired houses stress spatial quality over service, lifting daily life from the quotidian and specific to the timeless and universal. The simplicity of a small house gives it a head start on the pavilion ideal and its rewards in spaciousness and transcendence.

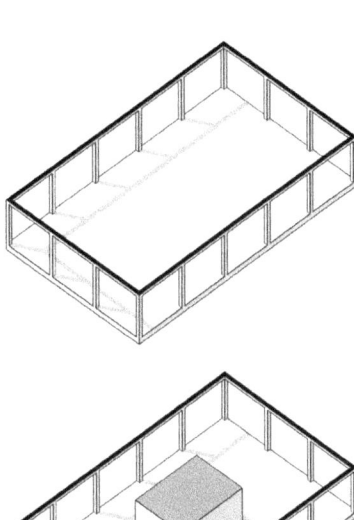

The pavilion prototype is a one-space, open-sided enclosure.

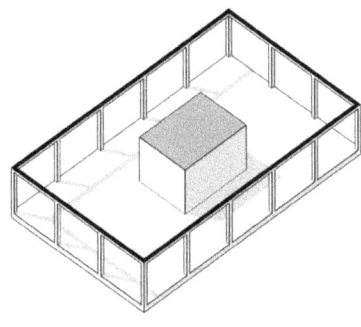

Pavilion homes like Mies's Farnsworth House and Philip Johnson's Glass House add modern conveniences in a service core that preserves the defining open perimeter of the hallmark single space. (See Example House B, p. 60.)

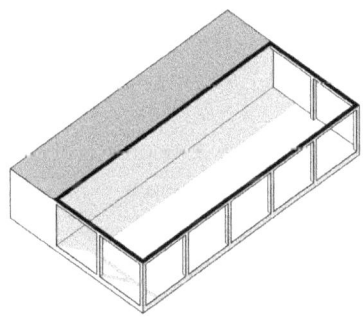

Services can also be added to a pavilion-based house by incorporating them in a thickened wall (Ch. 42) of what remains in effect a one-room building. (See Example House C, p. 88.)

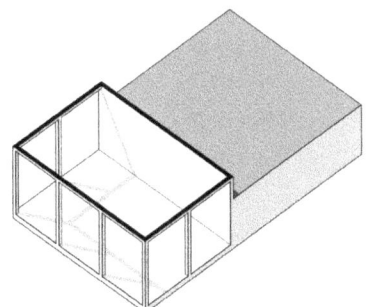

Even when a living area occupies the smaller part of a house's footprint, it can be prioritized with height and openness into a single dominant space, capturing the pavilion spirit. (See Example House A, p. 32.)

35 | One-Room Appeal

In 1872, the German philosopher Robert Vischer coined the word *einfühlung* — literally "feeling into" — to describe how we project emotions onto objects and phenomena like trees and storms. The psychologist Theodor Lipps refined the concept to include the way we identify with the feelings of others or find beauty in objects in which we see ourselves. In 1909, einfühlung was translated into English as "empathy."

We naturally see human qualities everywhere. Automotive designers anticipate our reactions to the facial expressions we'll read in car fronts. Symmetrical objects appeal to us by mirroring our own symmetry. When charmed by a small house, we're responding to its closeness to the scale of our bodies and projecting human warmth into it. This applies most to a house defined by a decisively main room. Like our body, it has one resident spirit. The celebrated architect Frank Gehry has spoken of "the power of one-room buildings and the fact that historically, the best buildings ever built are one-room buildings."

A dwelling needn't be a true pavilion like Philip Johnson's Glass House (Ch. 39, Ch. 47) to harness the power and unity of a one-room building. Even a house of many rooms can be unified by a clearly focal space. This is largely the role of the double-height great hall which gives a heart and sometimes even a namesake identity to English country houses like Hardwick Hall. The living space of a small house can serve this purpose if it's distinguished by height, light, views, spaciousness, and grandeur.

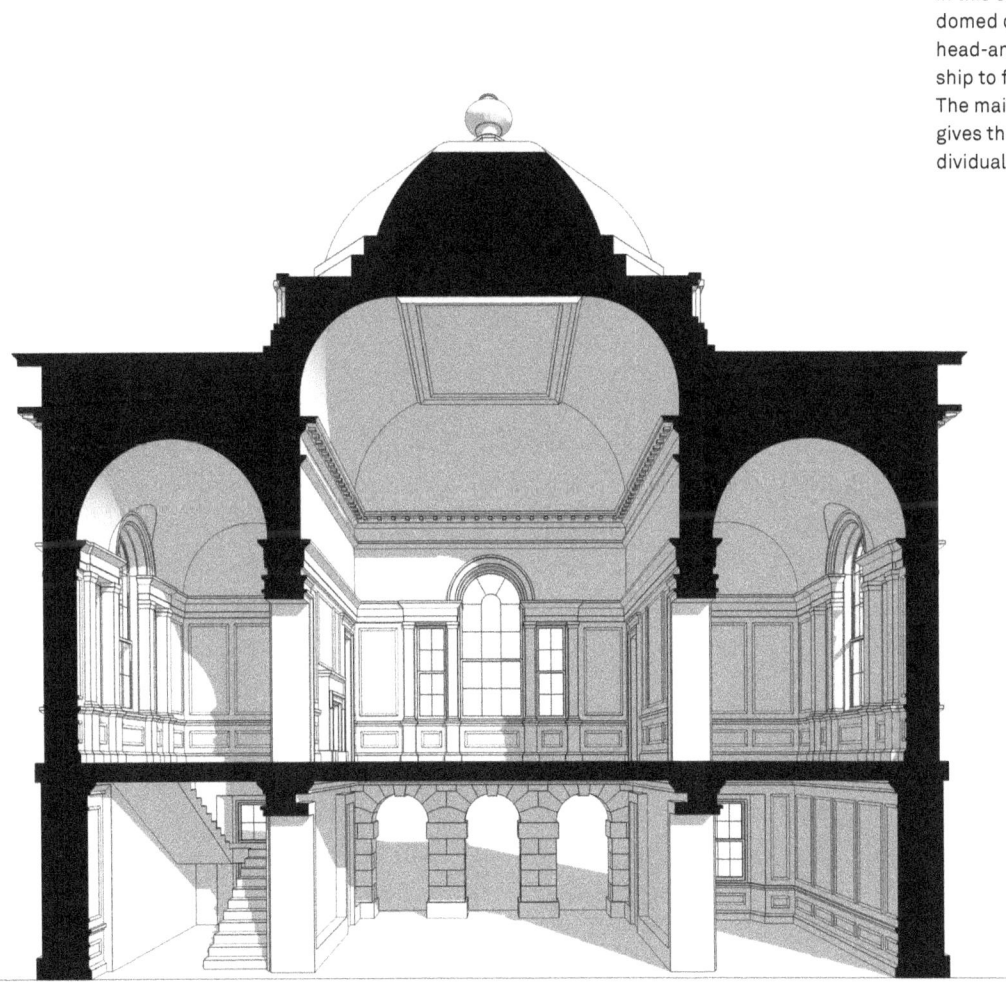

A perspective view generated from a design in James Gibbs's influential *Book of Architecture* (1728) shows a garden building which might well be a small house. From mansions to gazebos, the prototypes in Gibbs's pattern book have a single unifying main space. His humanizing intent is seen in this example's prioritized, domed central room with its head-and-shoulders relationship to flanking service wings. The main room's dominance gives the whole a relatable individuality and one-room spirit.

36 | Box

The Kanizsa Square illusion makes the eye see a non-existent square. The effect is so strong that we may sense ghost lines defining the sides of the square at their open midpoints, or the white square as brighter than its white "background." The illusion proves how powerfully corners define containing shapes, which are best avoided in a small house.

    Corners historically stabilized buildings and rooms by allowing perpendicular walls to prop each other up. Many traditional architectural styles are rooted in this structural imperative, which is primarily a vestige of masonry construction. Present-day building technology is less structurally reliant on the closed corner. Modern architecture celebrates the open corner, liberating space by "breaking the box" (Ch. 48).

    The Kanizsa illusion is a function of gestalt psychology, by which we grasp a thing in its entirety even when it isn't fully visible. Our safety depends constantly on this formation of split-second recognitions in a chaotic world of fragmentary evidence. It's a vital reflex—instant, involuntary, and forceful—that bends our mind to fill in gaps. If the gap is a door or window interrupting a wall plane, this reflex tries to restore the wall's integrity by negating any opening punched through it. This subconsciously diminishes its effect of spatial release. An opening near the middle of a wall between intact corners especially invites the mind to seal it up and complete the wall as our eye does the open sides of the Kanizsa Square (Ch. 24).

The psychologist Gaetano Kanizsa invented the Kanizsa Square and other demonstrations of "illusory contours."

37 | Box Breaking

The 1923 plan of Mies van der Rohe's Brick Country House project is one of modern architecture's iconic images. It was radical in its day for looking more like an abstract artwork than a house plan. This wasn't the kind of typical house Frank Lloyd Wright criticized as a box full of smaller boxes connected by holes punched through their walls.

Wright said he aimed in his houses "to eliminate the room as a box and the house as another by making all walls enclosing screens — the ceilings and floors and enclosing screens all flowing into each other as one large enclosure of space, with minor subdivisions only." We see Wright's influence in Mies's Country House plan. It attacks the box at its defining corners, rarely letting them suggest a conventional static room, trap space, or create a dead end. Almost all exterior-wall corners are broken open by floor-to-ceiling glass. This allows indoor space and — suggestively — even interior walls to flow into the landscape.

Throughout Mies's Country House plan, space seems freed from the confines of the conventional, container-like house Wright equated to a coffin. Even a compact house with a rectangular footprint can break the box by erasing its strong-point corners.

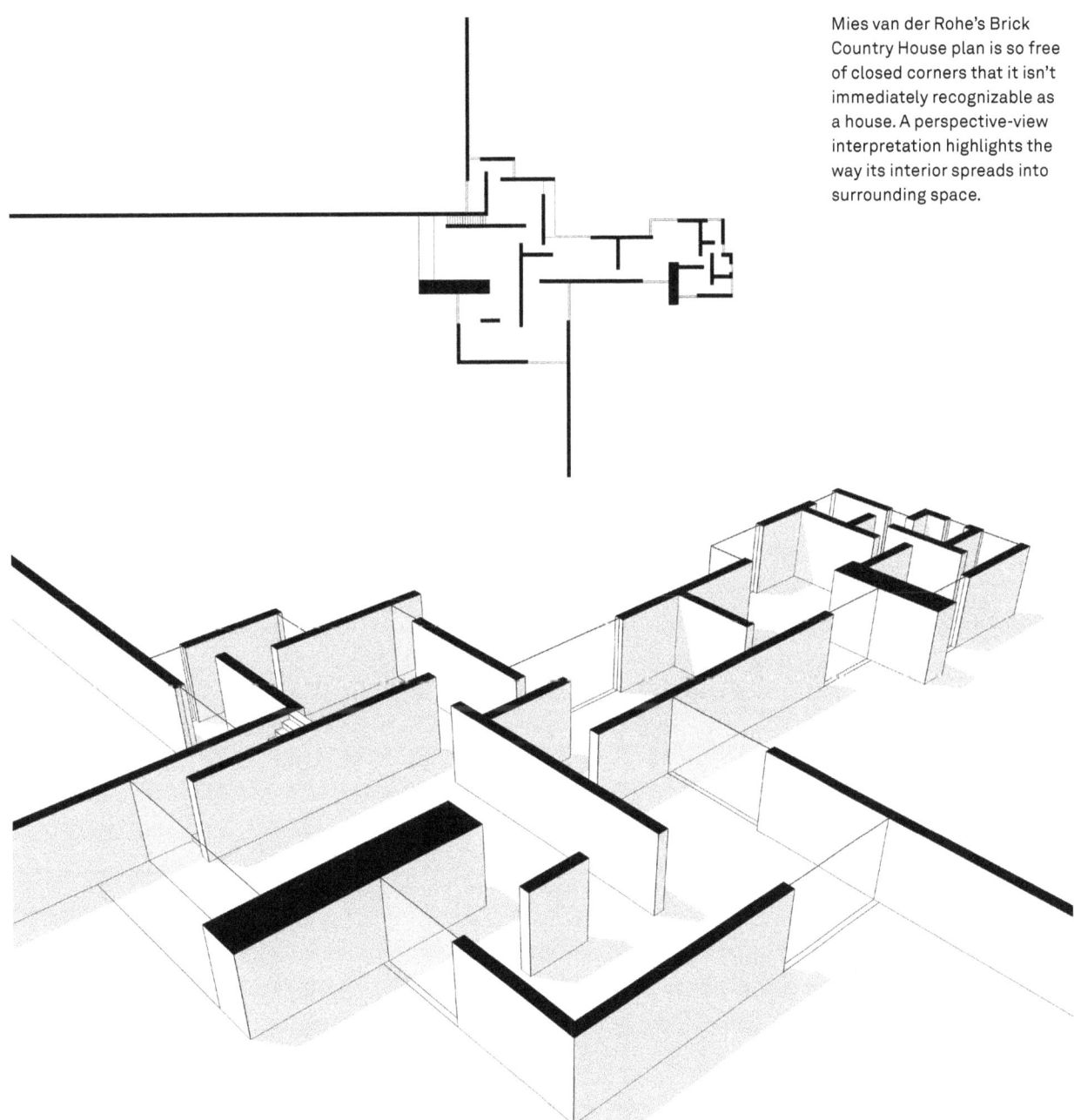

Mies van der Rohe's Brick Country House plan is so free of closed corners that it isn't immediately recognizable as a house. A perspective-view interpretation highlights the way its interior spreads into surrounding space.

38 | Endlessness

Mies van der Rohe's 1945–51 Farnsworth House redefined residential luxury as the simplest lifestyle and greatest intimacy with nature. It is a box broken open with glass not just at the corners like his Brick Country House project (Ch. 37) but around its entire perimeter. At 1,600 square feet, it's much smaller than today's typical American house. Its extreme simplicity and spaciousness hold suggestions for even smaller houses.

Mies went beyond Frank Lloyd Wright's combination of living activities in a single space (Ch. 14). He unified all functions except bathrooms and a mechanical closet, which aren't so much partitioned off as camouflaged within a furniture-like service island around which space flows in an endless loop. All space-trapping, opaque, inside corners are hidden within this core. With its doors distinguished from paneling only by their knobs and its walls stopping short of the main ceiling, it reads as a freestanding solid inserted within the single open volume of the house, preserving the overall effect of a spaciously undivided pavilion. A single-galley kitchen along one side of the core is shielded from view.

The Farnsworth House's roof and floor planes seem to just provisionally claim a section of infinite space (Ch. 13). Extending past the glass envelope at one end to create a porch, they blur the line between inside and out like the walls of the Brick Country House that extend into the landscape (Ch. 37). Open views are maximized within the house and beyond its walls, outdoing Wright in his pursuit of "vista without and vista within."

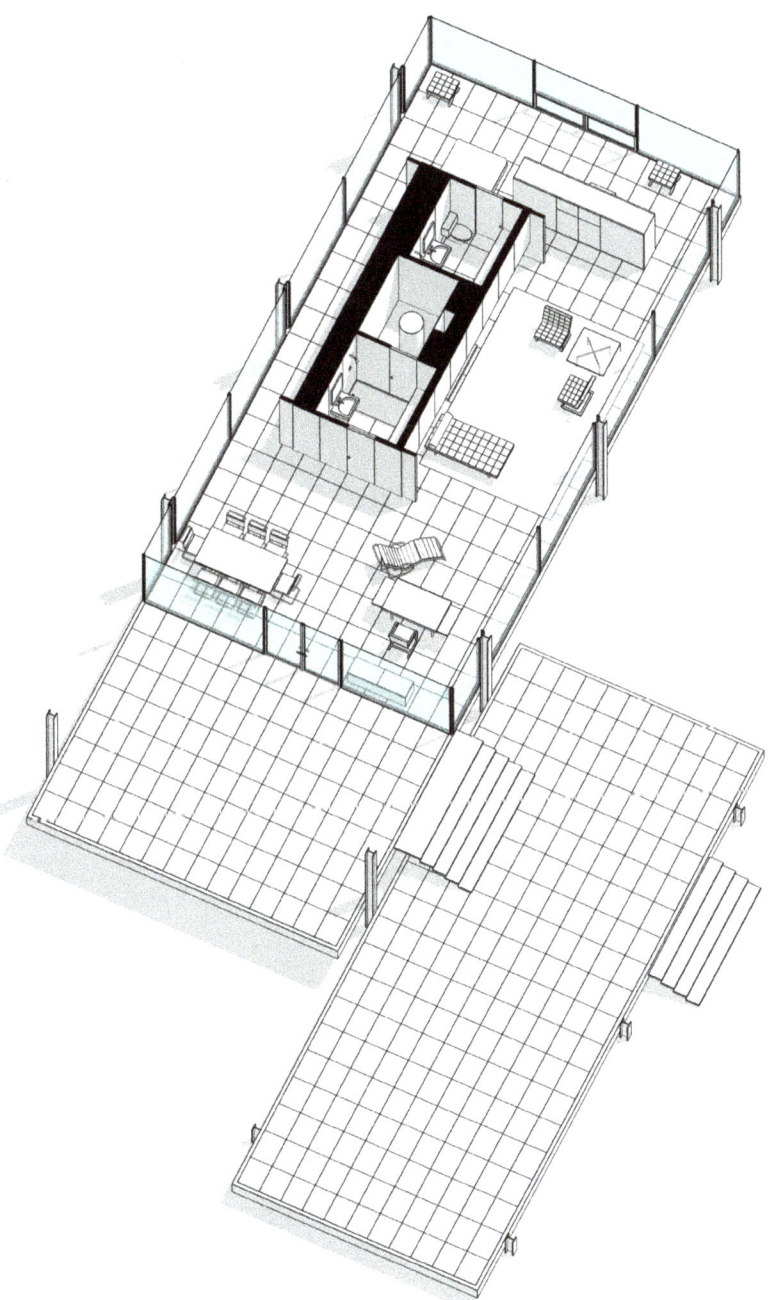

Philip Johnson said that when Mies first conceived of a glass house in 1945, "I pointed out to him that it was impossible because you had to have rooms, and that meant solid walls up against the glass, which ruined the whole point." Mies replied, "I think it can be done." His solution is far more than a means to an uninterrupted glass perimeter.

39 | Boundary

The legible perimeter of a house's open living area determines its maximum visually perceived interior scale, a critical consideration in the design of a small house. This boundary excludes separately enclosed spaces like bedrooms, bathrooms, or closets.

Mies van der Rohe's Farnsworth House (Ch. 38) and the Glass House it inspired Philip Johnson to build are extreme cases in which this perimeter is the full extent of the house's interior, creating the maximum possible impression of size. As islands, their freestanding service cores don't reduce this extent any more than Hawaii does the Pacific's, because the outer limit is unaffected. This kind of open plan was the prerogative of singles like Johnson or Mies's client, Dr. Edith Farnsworth, and could serve many current American households, most of which consist of an individual or couple.

Though clearly derivative of the Farnsworth House, the Glass House takes its radical openness even further. The cylindrical core housing its bathroom and fireplace is a much smaller proportion of the house footprint, allowing a more nearly 360-degree grasp of the space-defining interior perimeter and surrounding nature. Its shape makes it appear even more as inserted — and thus mentally removable — than Mies's rectangular core. Endless, liberated space loops more fluidly around its curved surface. Its geometry better distinguishes it from, and stresses by contrast, the simplifying unity of the house's raft-like floor. It also allows the continuity of the scale-setting perimeter to be more clearly inferred even where passing out of sight behind the core.

Philip Johnson fully acknowledged the debt his 1949 Glass House owed Mies's earlier-conceived but later-built Farnsworth House. It is only the first of the Farnsworth's many celebrated progeny.

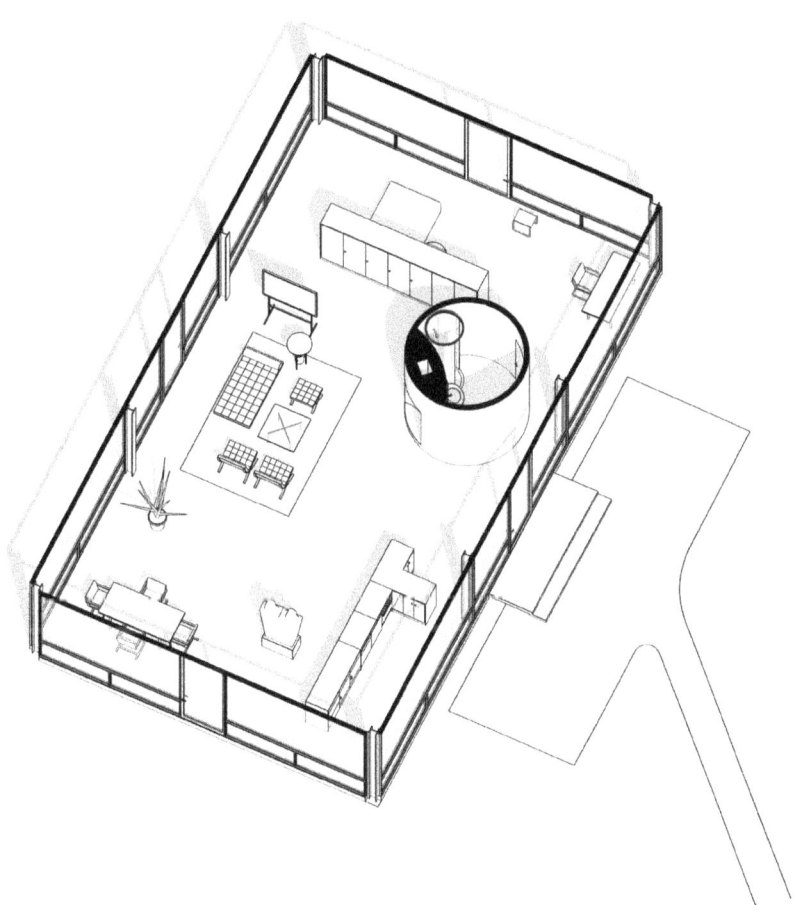

40 | Clarity

Stalked by stealthy predators, early man passed his wariness of the unseen on to us. Horror movies exploit this, banking on our visceral reaction to many-roomed mansions, cobwebby basements, alien or prehistoric pursuers, and the shock of surprise attack. As if to keep our guard up, our imagination posits threats from hidden spaces beyond the modern equivalent of the ancestral campfire's circle of light. Even when we know nothing's hiding in unseen spaces around us, they trouble us subconsciously.

The coziness of the child's improvised playhouse lies in its ability to be defensibly taken in all at once. Thoreau wrote in *Walden* (Ch. 29) that he sometimes dreamed of a one-room house (Ch. 35) "whose inside is as open and manifest as a bird's nest." A simple house can approach this ideal. Attaching a garage, basement, second story, or any unnecessary room fights it.

Snake-detection theory, developed by anthropologist Lynne Isbell, holds that the visual acuity of primates evolved in response to snakes, which had earlier evolved to be hard to detect and mortally dangerous. Our ability to quickly identify such dangers within a complex visual environment is vital. Reducing an interior's unnecessary distractions reassures us in much the same way as removing out-of-sight secondary spaces. It also allows objects "blissfully few and adorably good" in Henry James's words to stand out and define a house's quality. According to Dieter Rams, "One of the most significant design principles is to omit the unimportant in order to emphasize the important."

To make any thing very terrible, obscurity seems in general to be necessary. When we know the full extent of any danger, when we can accustom our eyes to it, a great deal of the apprehension vanishes. Every one will be sensible of this, who considers how greatly night adds to our dread, in all cases of danger, and how much the notions of ghosts and goblins, of which none can form clear ideas, affect minds, which give credit to the popular tales concerning such sorts of beings.

Edmund Burke, *A Philosophical Enquiry into the Origin of our Ideas of the Sublime and Beautiful*

But our reason telling us that there is no danger does not suffice. I may mention a trifling fact, illustrating this point, and which at the time amused me. I put my face close to the thick glass plate in front of a puff-adder in the Zoological Gardens, with the firm determination of not starting back if the snake struck at me: but as soon as the blow was struck, my resolution went for nothing, and I jumped a yard or two backwards with astonishing rapidity. My will and reason were powerless against the imagination of a danger which had never been experienced.

Charles Darwin, *The Expression of the Emotions in Man and Animals*

Example

D

32' x 26'
832 square feet
12' & 7' ceilings

As in Example C, the front of this house is a thickened wall containing entry hall, bathroom, and storage, but here an enclosed bedroom as well. Here too, the front service zone buffers the private living area from the street. The bedroom can share its volume and light with the main space of the house, preserving the ideal of a one-room dwelling. It is separated from the living area by low bookshelves between vertical fins which extend to the ceiling, supporting the roof. These fins also serve as tracks for vertically sliding shutter panels to seal the bedroom off at night. By day, the shutters are drawn down behind the bookshelves, which screen the bed from the living area's view and remain open above. This allows the living area to borrow the bedroom's space, natural light, and sky-and-tree views through its privately high front windows above the bed. Lower windows flanking the bed provide the emergency escape required by code for bedrooms. Abundant light from the front of the house balances that from the rear bank of sliding glass doors with transoms, which achieves a wall-to-wall window effect with the help of alcoves at either end of the living space (Section C-C, p. 123).

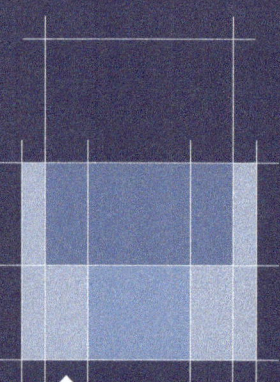

Example D

Plan

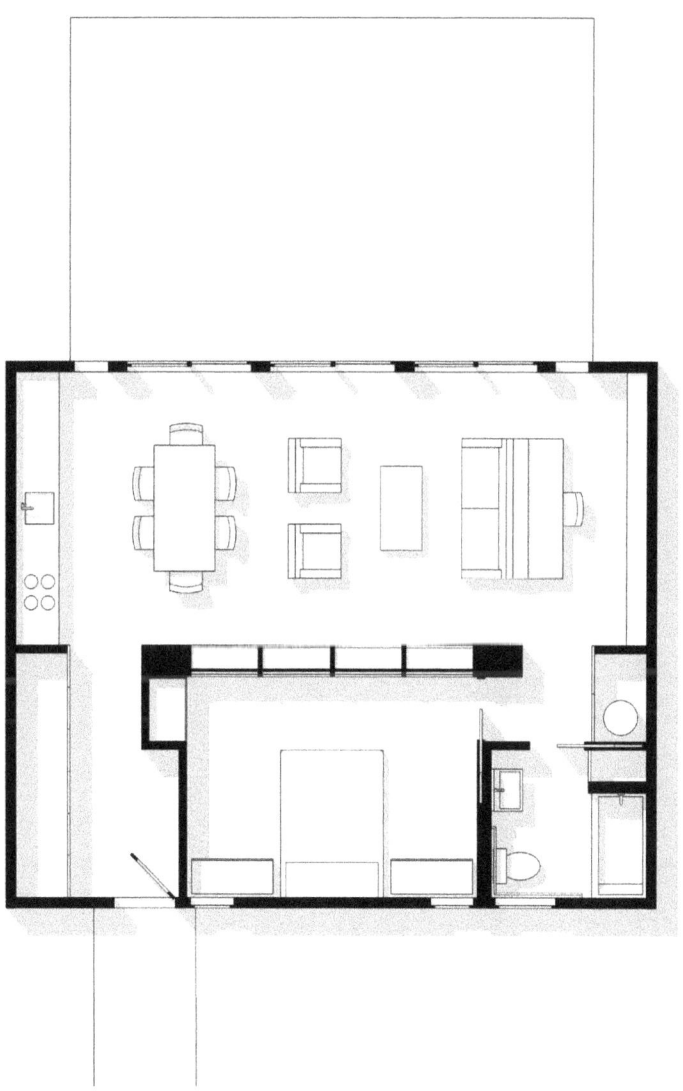

Example D
Low plan perspective from front

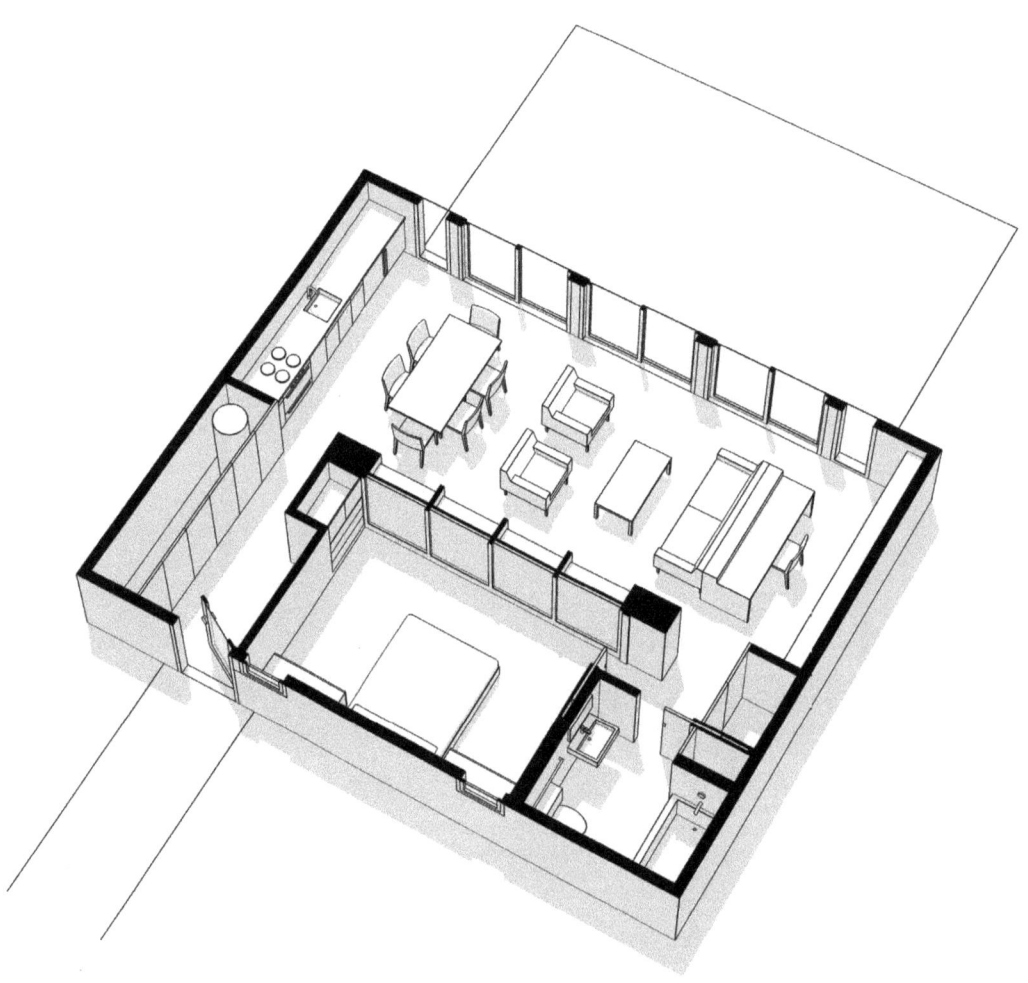

Example D
High plan perspective from rear

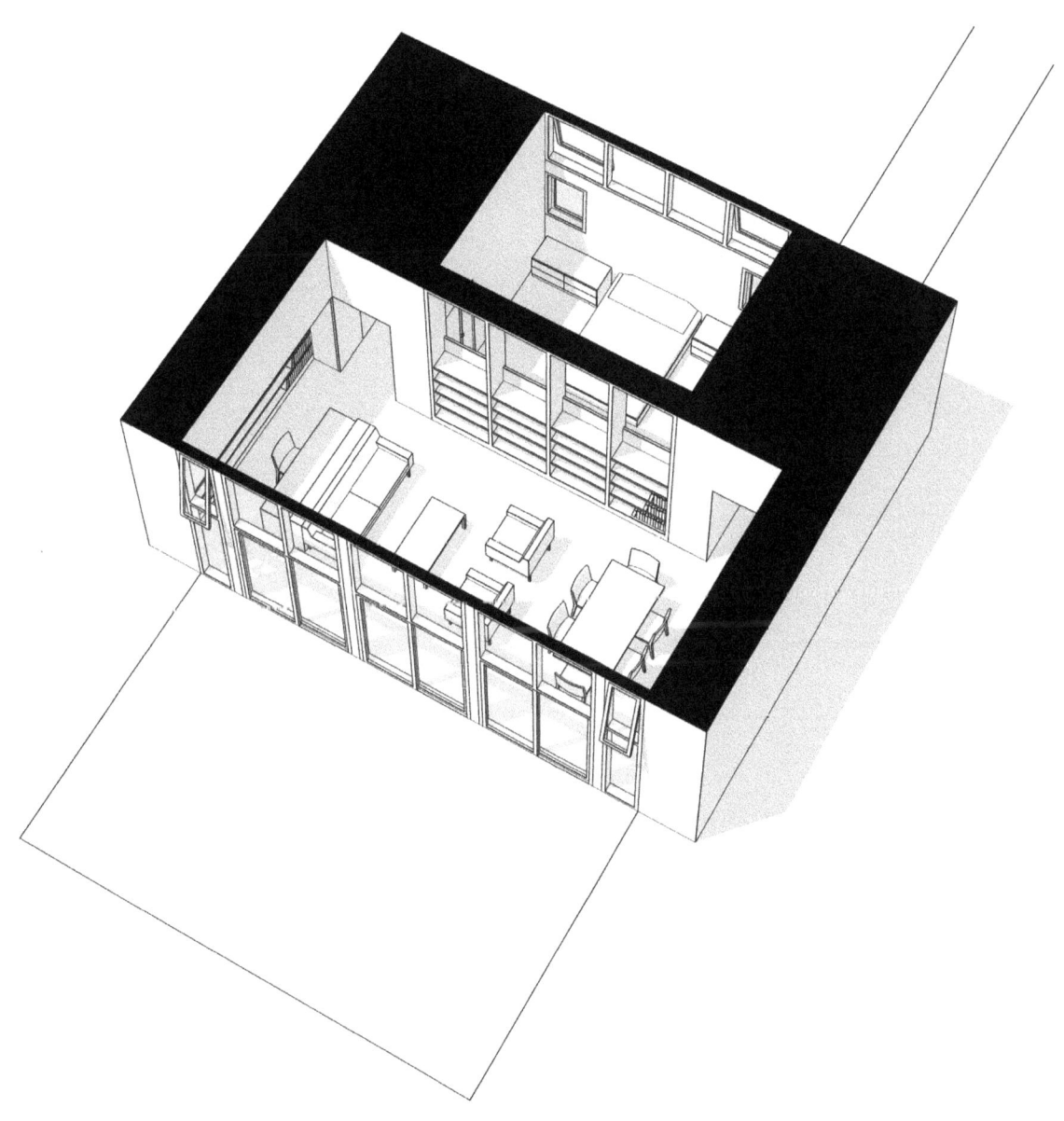

Example D
Front

Example D
Rear

Example D
Top: Section key plan
Bottom: Section B-B

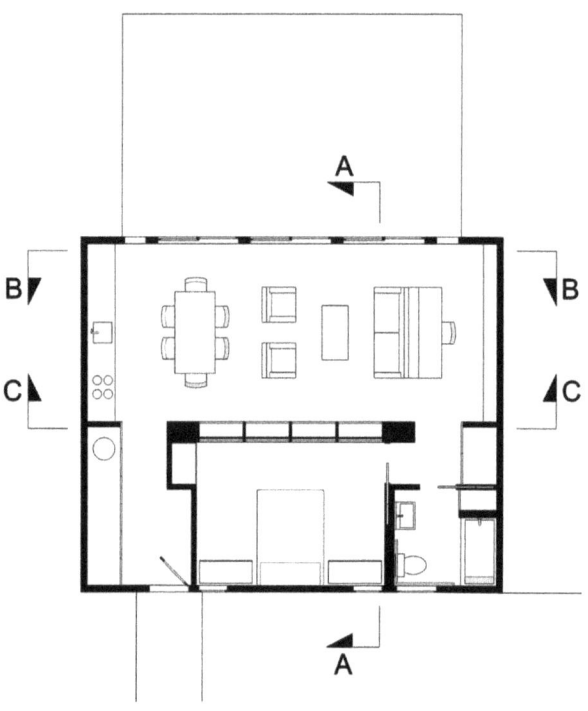

Example D
Top: Section A-A
Bottom: Section C-C

41 | Served and Servant

Louis Kahn brought a spiritual sensibility to the functionalism of modern architecture. He appreciated the soaring ceiling of ancient Rome's Baths of Caracalla for going "beyond function."

Kahn's buildings make peace between timeless monumentality and intrusive modern services through his concept of "served" and "servant" space. Rather than starting the design process with the glory work of laying out perfect primary spaces, later to compromise them with utilities and support spaces as an afterthought, Kahn gave equal weight to both aspects of a building from its conception. He said "The architect must find a way in which the serving areas of a space can be there, and still not destroy his spaces." He found his solution in the design-by-diagram approach Palladio employed to lay out his villas, which gave both major and minor spaces their place at once (Ch. 43).

Kahn's seminal Trenton Bath House design originated from a "tartan plaid" diagram that collects serving spaces in narrow zones and more public, served spaces in broad ones. Kahn elevated this banded-diagram approach, evident in early American dwellings (Ch. 7) and many of Frank Lloyd Wright's houses (Ch. 14, Ch. 43), to a first principle, using it to retain the old architectural values of integrity, order, clarity, and grandeur even as they were being displaced by increasingly complex service technologies.

The served-and-servant strategy can grant a small house the idealized simplicity and mythic resonance of the primitive hut or pavilion while incorporating modern conveniences.

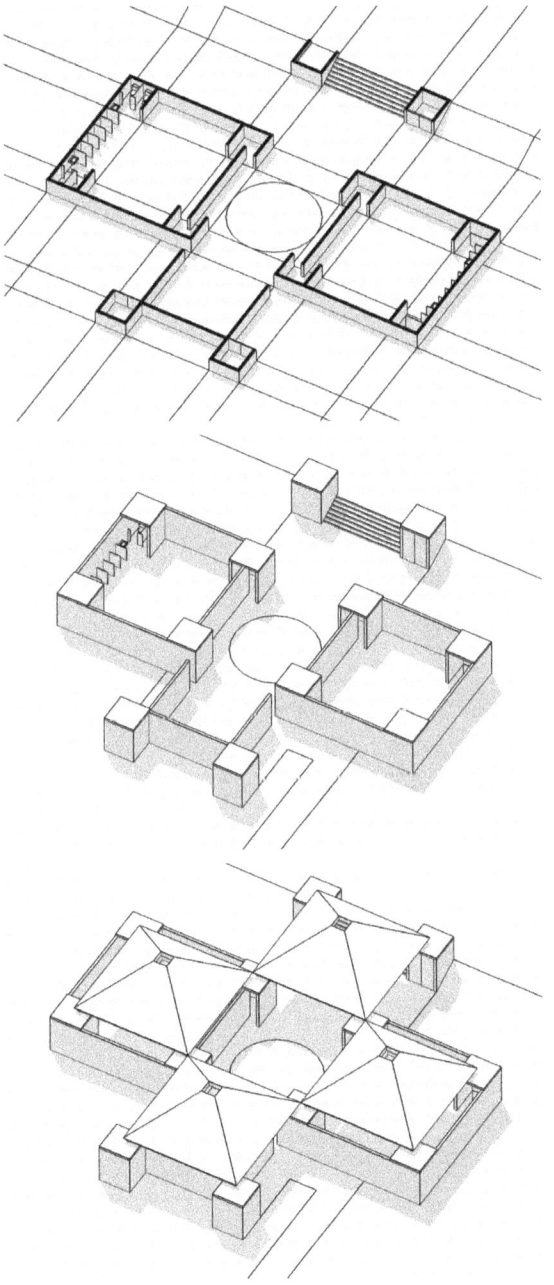

The plan diagram of Louis Kahn's Trenton Bath House organizes services in narrow bands (top). Their intersections form storage spaces, toilets, and entrances with sightline baffles to male and female shower pavilions. These small squares are topped by concrete slabs (middle) which hold up the corners of four roofs (bottom), adding structural support to their "servant" role. The diagram reconciles multiple practical demands with the simple image of a cluster of one-room, hut-like pavilions. Each has a pyramidal roof truncated by an oculus recalling the Pantheon's (p. 9). They surround a central, circular gravel pit nodding to the plan of Palladio's Villa Rotonda (p. 8). Kahn's diagram-based approach exalts a utilitarian building with the power of archetypes.

42 | Thickened Wall

A modernist taken with the emotional power and sense of eternity in past architecture, Louis Kahn said, "I have a book of castles and I try to pretend that I did not look at this book but everyone reminds me of it and I have to admit that I looked very thoroughly at this book. It was so inspiring to see these thick walls and the gift that is given to the interior of the space." Kahn noted how the thickened walls of castles absorb support spaces so "the central area is given to you in a most wonderful way."

This strategy, which Kahn adapted to his own buildings, is closely related to his diagram-based design approach and concept of served and servant space (Ch. 41). The castle's thick walls are effectively diagrammatic service zones. In seeming to be part of the wall thickness, support spaces recede and give primacy to the simple rectangle of the central hall, allowing a satisfying correspondence between the building's exterior and interior.

The castle example can be applied to the design of a small house by conceiving a purely shaped living area served and embraced on one or more sides by thickened walls containing support spaces like bedrooms, bathroom, and closets. This can give the house the primal power and unified identity of a one-room building.

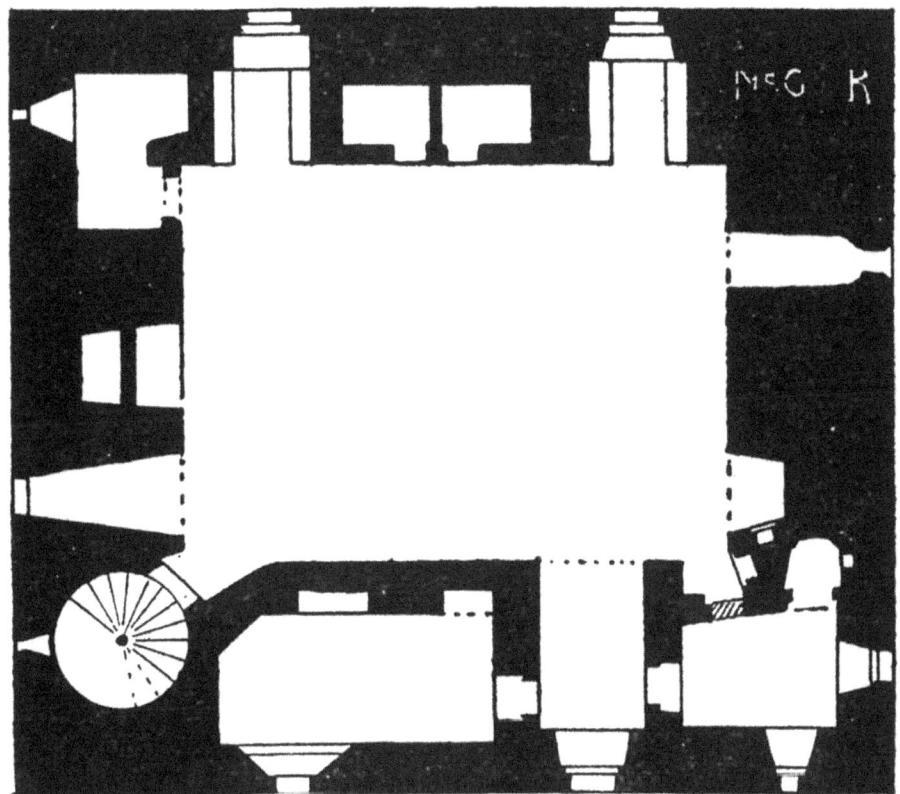

Kahn lectured using floor plans of Comlongon Castle from the 1887 survey, *The Castellated and Domestic Architecture of Scotland from the Twelfth to the Eighteenth Century* by David MacGibbon and Thomas Ross.

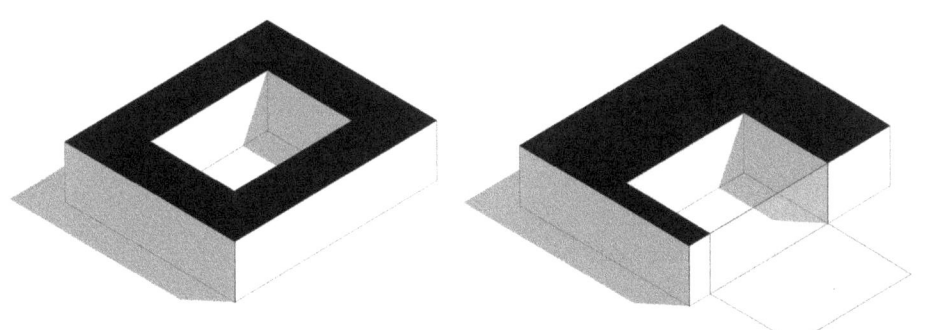

Adapted to the design of a small house, the open core of such a plan can be made the living area and opened up to the exterior, imparting a one-room sensibility.

43 | Diagram

Designing from a whole-house diagram ensures integrity. The diagram should be as simple as possible, organizing the floor plan into service zones for support functions and passageways, and larger zones for the main spaces they serve. It should respond to interior needs and spatial relationships, and external site forces like path of approach, views, privacy, topography, and orientation to sun, wind, and noise.

The diagrammatic approach contrasts with that of the designer who plants rooms in sequence across a house, one decision limiting the next, with each successive function more awkwardly forced into leftover space. This yields the quagmire of many a tract house plan, burdened with room shapes no one would ever deliberately design from scratch but could only have backed into, painted into a corner. A comprehensive diagram accommodating every function results not only in perfect individual spaces but the most efficient overall plan.

A simple small-house diagram will produce a clear design made up of simultaneously conceived spaces that are all deliberate, vital, and whole. The clarity, simplicity, and harmony of the house's conception will come through in the final product's sense of serene refuge. A diagram-based house's economical compactness can offset the cost of grandeur-imparting features (Ch. 46).

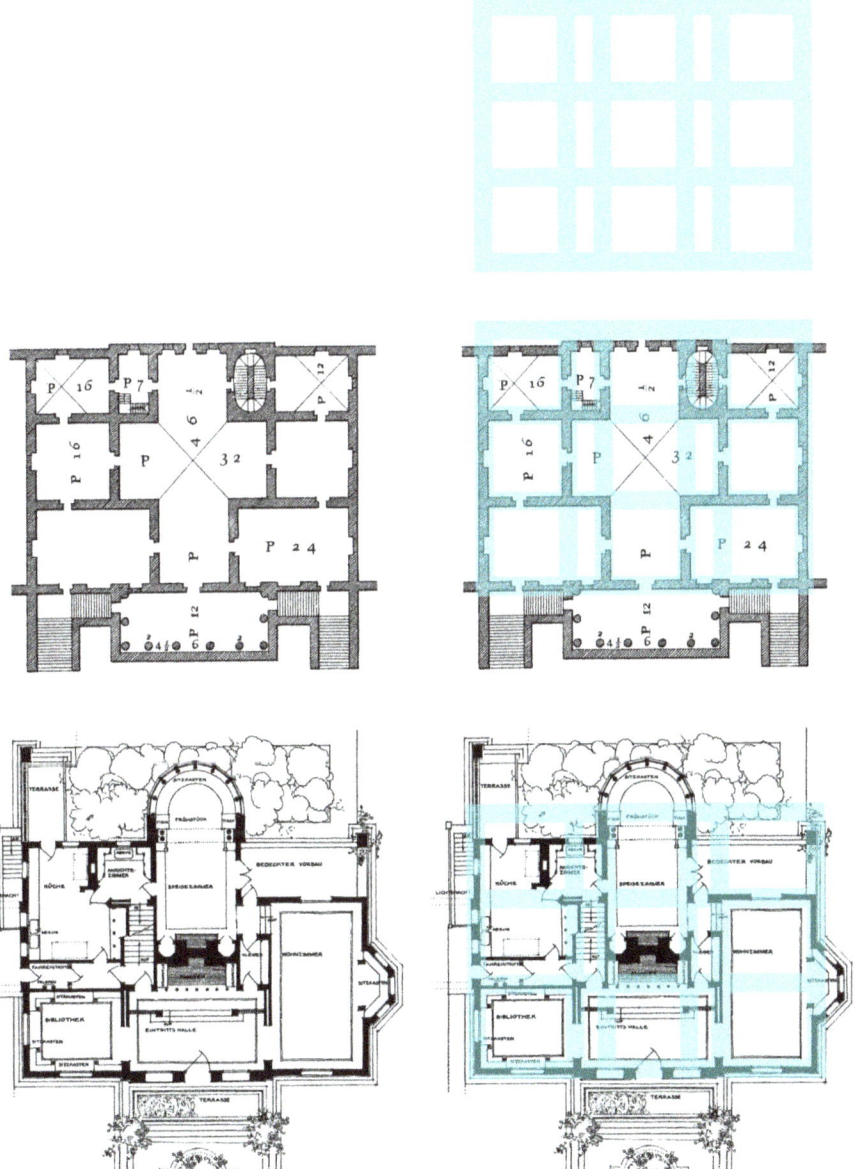

Rudolph Wittkower's 1949 book, *Architectural Principles in the Age of Humanism*, identified a simple grid pattern underlying eleven villas by the supremely influential Renaissance architect, Andrea Palladio. It's here superimposed not just on the plan of Palladio's Villa Foscari (1558–60), but on Frank Lloyd Wright's 1893 Winslow House (bottom) where it deftly integrates services — kitchen, pantry, stairs, driveway entrance, and storage — without compromising the shape or organization of the house's living spaces. Louis Kahn was fascinated by Wittkower's analysis and applied it to his concept of served and servant spaces (Ch. 41).

44 | Privacy

Windows that brighten a small house and make it feel larger may also reduce privacy. An awareness of this problem should inform a house's generative diagram and determine where its envelope is transparent.

On an economically compact building lot, next-door houses or their future likelihood call for side façades with few or no windows. As opaque buffers, these blank sides may usefully be thickened into storage walls and places for alcoves. Front windows placed high enough can ensure privacy from more distant across-the-street houses while allowing generous treetop and sky views. High ceilings and windows allow not only private views above neighbors, but deeper penetration of natural light and greater exposure of the sky canopy, helping simulate outdoor experience. Translucent glazing can secure privacy while providing illumination and exterior spatial release as we sense outdoor daylight and activity through it.

Our ancestral need for concealment from predators and protection from surprise attack lives on in us as an acute sensitivity to privacy. Modern neighbors may pose no threat, but most of the time we're more comfortable out of their view and vice versa. A house's entry door compromises privacy by its very potential to open, and is best shielded or set apart by a transition space from the living area. Interior doors opening directly onto a living area from other spaces can also diminish its spirit of tranquil private refuge and should be minimized.

A front wall with high windows above a kitchen provides sky views and abundant light while screening across-the-street neighbors and traffic. A blank side wall gives privacy from a nearby next-door neighbor. The private back invites the most open exposure. (Example House A, p. 32.)

45 | Time

One of the best reasons to build a small, simple house is to free up time for living. The less time spent maintaining a home or working to pay for it, the more there is to enjoy life. Thoreau saw house and life as reciprocal, one growing as the other shrinks. Feeding our inherited compulsion to stockpile and display doesn't deliver happiness. Time well spent does. In the end, our lives are measured in accumulated experiences and relationships, not possessions which mock our mortality when we can't take them with us.

Building a house with a simple footprint and efficiently diagrammed floor plan on an affordably small lot will contain its cost and demands on freedom. Adding an element of strategically deployed grandeur will add to its cost but make a worthwhile difference in quality of free time at home and appreciation of everyday life.

Building with durable materials that weather attractively is one way to keep a house from stealing our time over its life cycle. Another is simplicity of form, which limits operating expenses. Compact building shells cost less to heat and cool. Building envelopes tend to fail at their construction joints, especially intersecting surface planes. Limiting a house to four walls and a roof saves money over a house's — and our own — life cycle, while satisfying our innate desire for clarity and simplicity.

I had three pieces of limestone on my desk, but I was terrified to find that they required to be dusted daily, when the furniture of my mind was all undusted still, and I threw them out the window in disgust. How then could I have a furnished house? I would rather sit in the open air, for no dust gathers on the grass, unless where man has broken ground.... A man is rich in proportion to the number of things which he can afford to let alone.

Henry David Thoreau, *Walden*

46 | Grandeur

A house doesn't need a large footprint to have grandeur, which can best be achieved by giving the living area a high ceiling that evokes the loftiness of nature and tall windows that admit the real thing. Distinguishing its main space this way also gives a house a unified identity. Most of us spend the great majority of our waking hours at home in one favorite room, a lion's share of time which deserves a commensurate setting.

It's a long-held article of faith in the architectural profession that a designer can create more value out of thin air by shaping space than through costly detailing or materials. In the introduction to *A Book of Architecture* (Ch. 35), James Gibbs explained: "For it is not the bulk of a fabric, the richness and quantity of the materials, the multiplicity of lines, that give the grace or beauty and grandeur to a building; but the proportion of the parts to one another and the whole, whether entirely plain, or enriched with a few ornaments properly disposed."

Grandeur can be financed with what's saved by building an otherwise economical and compact house. Outdoor-simulating verticality and openness don't come free, but they add nothing to a house's square footage and little or nothing to the cost of its foundation, roof, appliances, fixtures, wiring, plumbing, or furniture, while enormously amplifying its sense of space. Inspired house design skews common priorities to uncommon ends, saving radically here to transcend the ordinary there, and tapping the contrast for drama.

Charles Moore said his 1961 Bonham House "though tiny and economical, possesses great apparent size." Its double-height main room's giant factory window tilts back as if craning to take in the surrounding redwoods and sky, co-opting the scale of nature for the 567-square-foot house. An oversized stair landing holds the bed, and the space below it a fireplace pit. Inspired by the writings of Sir John Summerson (Ch. 47), these snug spaces might have been appropriated by children playing house. "A kind of dream grandeur comes from the constant juxtaposition of the spacious and the close," Moore noted, echoing James Gibbs's case that grandeur is a matter of proportion. (Photograph by Morley Baer. ©2019 The Morley Baer Photography Trust, Santa Fe. All rights reserved. Used by permission.)

47 | Passion

"I'd rather live in the nave of Chartres Cathedral and go out of doors to the john," Philip Johnson said. We identify with him when we stand in a forest glade or sublime ruin and dream of living there. Though quickly silenced by grownup reason, this inner-child voice exposes our discontent with the numbingly convenient and its cost in wonder.

The grandeur of Chartres's forest of branching Gothic columns is recalled in the tree canopy above Johnson's Glass House, which seems to camp out below. Sir John Summerson's essay "Heavenly Mansions" sums up its emotional allure:

> None of us ever entirely outgrows the love of the doll's house or, usually in a vicarious form, the love of squatting under the table. Camping and sailing are two adult forms of play analogous to the "my house" pretenses of a child. In both, there is the fascination of the miniature shelter which excludes the elements by only a narrow margin and intensifies the sense of security in a hostile world.

Johnson's home differs most from the floodplain-raised Farnsworth House (Ch. 13), which inspired it, in resting on the ground. This better imparts the simple power of the primitive hut or pavilion and gives its floor an expansive continuity with the surrounding ground plane. Johnson seems to have heeded Thoreau's advice to "consider first how slight a shelter is absolutely necessary." Excluding all but a lovingly selected handful of furniture and art pieces, the Glass House has the appeal of a play-house refuge.

The architecture historian Vincent Scully said of Philip Johnson's 1949 Glass House, "I think it's one of the most important buildings in America. The Glass House is a real archetype — a fundamental piece of architecture, like a life support pod — and as such it is full of suggestions for the future."

48 | Modernism

A traditional small house that oozes charm from the outside may feel disappointingly cramped inside. Older styles are driven by picturesque, surface concerns, focusing more on the container than the contained. Their formulas favor our material bias over our freedom bias, thwarting adventurous exploration of spatial potential. In his 1904 book, *Apollo*, the archaeologist and humanist Salomon Reinach wrote: "In the conflict that obtains between the two elements of architecture, solidity and open space, everything seems to show that the principle of free space will prevail, that the palaces and houses of the future will be flooded with air and light."

Modern architecture's box-breaking emphasis on openness, flowing space, and natural light allows it to make more of a small house than any earlier style. While modernism is itself a period style of the twentieth century, many of its tenets are universal. In focusing on timeless qualities of experience rather than physical substance and jettisoning the baggage of historical association, it allows for a more liberating small house that best captures the spirit of the getaway. Modernism originally focused on problems of the common man, tackling issues like worker housing and aiming to improve life for all. This democratic history is still seen in its prioritization of free light and space.

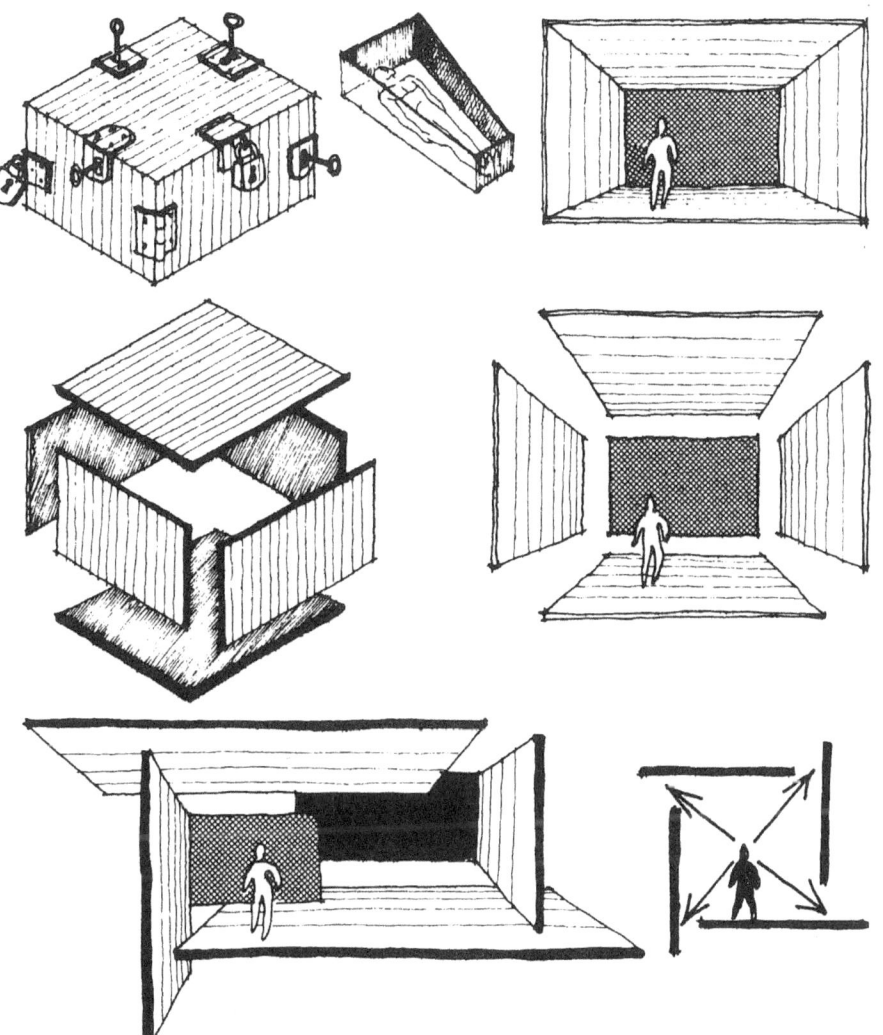

Bruno Zevi illustrated his 1978 book *The Modern Language of Architecture* with this cluster of images. His caption reads: "The box encloses, confining one like in a coffin. But if we separate the box's six planes, we have performed the revolutionary act of modern architecture. The panels can be lengthened or shortened to vary the light in fluid spaces." Zevi's imagery recalls a long line of warnings against houses that bury us and suggests an alternative. (Courtesy Bruno Zevi Foundation.)

49 | Timelessness

In 1927, Daimler-Benz posed a young woman styled as a flapper with one of its Mercedes roadsters for a promotional photo in front of a new double house by Le Corbusier in the carmaker's hometown of Stuttgart. The racy model and streamlined building put the sports car in fast company, burnishing its aura of stripped-down, cutting-edge daring. The architecture remains of-the-moment because Le Corbusier's building blocks were timeless: light, air, and elementary shapes.

Timelessness adds to a small home's sense of refuge, allowing an escape from the crushing banality of our milieu—the commercial materialism and ephemera that distract us from the wonder of existence and would trivialize us to products of our generation, like the dated décor, fashions, hairstyles, cars, and attitudes of a claustrophobic period film.

Stripped down at the beach, we leave time behind. Sun on skin, wind in hair, sand between toes, waves buoying us on their eternal rhythm, we return home to nature. Under water, the mammalian diving reflex inherited from aquatic ancestors lets us to go longer between breaths than we can on land. Far from the sterility decried by modern architecture's critics, such sensuous immersion in perennial nature was Le Corbusier's inspiration. He swam twice a day from *le Cabanon*, his 12' × 14'-4" summer cabin on the Mediterranean. "I'm so comfortable in my cabanon that I'll probably end my days here," he foretold. Like Thoreau's cabin at Walden Pond, it was designed "to front only on the essential facts of life."

Le Corbusier dedicated part of his 1923 manifesto *Toward an Architecture* to the inspiration architects should take from the automobile. Daimler-Benz returned his compliment with this image. Corbusier's call for a house that is a "machine for living in" wasn't literal, or his houses would now look like industrial relics. It had to do with the precision and clarity of expression shared by a work of automotive engineering and a Greek temple, each the product of a rational selection process. He wrote that "selection means discarding, pruning, cleansing; making the Essential stand out anew stripped and clear."

50 | Less Is More

Mies van der Rohe's motto "less is more" partly relates to his concept of "universal space" designed for no one use and thus granted unlimited flexibility. This blank-slate concept would be prosaic if it didn't also poetically rescue space from servitude and allow it be profound, or foreground human freedom and potential. The Thoreau of "Our life is frittered away by detail.... Simplify, simplify" might add: "less detail is more life" or "less house is more freedom."

"Less but better" is the motto of Mies's kindred spirit and Apple's product-design inspiration, Dieter Rams, who argues:

> Good design is as little design as possible. The aim of design reduction is by no means the sterile sparseness that I and other like-minded designers have been accused of producing. Instead it is the freedom from the dominance of "things." … My aim is to leave out everything superfluous in order to allow the essential to come through. The resulting forms will be calm, pleasant, understandable and long lived.

The fewer and simpler a house's elements and contents, the more they grow in impact. We ourselves feel reciprocally expansive in environments approaching Shelley's beloved "waste and solitary places where we taste the pleasure of believing what we see is boundless, as we wish our souls to be."

In the arena of "as little design as possible," each decision looms — all the more reason to engage a skilled architect. As Mies also said, "God is in the details."

> We said there warn't no home like a raft, after all. Other places do seem so cramped up and smothery, but a raft don't. You feel mighty free and easy and comfortable on a raft.

Mark Twain, *The Adventures of Huckleberry Finn*

Selected Bibliography

James S. Ackerman, *Palladio*. New York: Penguin, 1966; reprint, 1991.

Jay Appleton, *The Experience of Landscape*. 1975; new edition, Hull: Univ. of Hull Press, 1986.

Kent C. Bloomer and Charles W. Moore, *Body, Memory and Architecture*. New Haven: Yale Univ. Press, 1977.

Theodore M. Brown, "Thoreau's Prophetic Architectural Program," *New England Quarterly* 38.1 (1965) 3-20.

Ross Chapin, *Pocket Neighborhoods: Creating Small-Scale Community in a Large-Scale World*. Newtown, CT: Taunton, 2011.

Robert Geddes, *The Forest Edge*. London: Architectural Design / New York: St. Martin's, 1982.

James Gibbs, *A Book of Architecture*. 1782; Mineola, NY: Dover, 2008.

Grant Hildebrand, *The Wright Space: Pattern & Meaning in Frank Lloyd Wright's Houses*. Seattle: Univ. of Washington Press, 1991.

Stover Jenkins and David Mohney, *The Houses of Philip Johnson*. New York: Abbeville, 2001.

Charles Moore, Gerald Allen, and Donlyn Lyndon, *The Place of Houses*. Berkeley: Univ. of California Press, 1974; new edition, 2000.

Daniel Nettle, *Happiness: The Science behind Your Smile*. New York: Oxford Univ. Press, 2006.

Steven Park, *Le Corbusier Redrawn: The Houses*. New York: Princeton Architectural Press, 2012.

Joseph Rykwert, *On Adam's House in Paradise: The Idea of the Primitive Hut in Architectural History*. Cambridge: MIT Press, 1972; 2nd edition, 1981.

Miles David Samson, *Hut Pavilion Shrine: Architectural Archetypes in Mid-Century Modernism*. Burlington, VT: Ashgate, 2015.

Henry David Thoreau, *Walden; or, Life in the Woods*. 1854; New York: Oxford Univ. Press, 2009.

John Summerson, *Heavenly Mansions and Other Essays on Architecture*. 1949; New York: Norton, 1998.

Maritz Vandenberg, *Farnsworth House*. New York: Phaidon, 2003.

Frank Lloyd Wright, *Ausgeführte Bauten und Entwürfe von Frank Lloyd Wright*. (Wasmuth Portfolio.) 1910; translated as *Drawings and Plans of Frank Lloyd Wright: The Early Period (1893-1909)*, Mineola, NY: Dover, 1983.

——. *The Natural House*. 1954; reprinted in *The Essential Frank Lloyd: Critical Writings on Architecture*, edited by Bruce Brooks Pfeiffer, Princeton: Princeton Univ. Press, 2009. Pp. 319–64.

Photo Credits

Author: 6 top & bottom, 10, 23, 45, 79, and 137

English Wikipedia, originally updated by user: Shward103, p. 85

Morley Baer. ©2019 The Morley Baer Photography Trust, Santa Fe. All rights reserved. Used by permission: 135

Stefan Bauer / CC-BY-SA-2.5 (http://creativecommons.org/licenses/by-sa/2.5/): 5

Library of Congress, Prints & Photographs Division, CONN, 2-HARF, 16–14: 43 top

The Mark Twain House & Museum, Hartford, Connecticut: 43 bottom

Mercedes-Benz Classic: 141

Xauxa / CC-BY-SA-3.0 (http://creativecommons.org/licenses/by-sa/3.0/): 27

www.ingramcontent.com/pod-product-compliance
Lightning Source LLC
Chambersburg PA
CBHW042035100526
44587CB00030B/4433